A Modern Shaman Speaks...

Shamanic Depossession

A Compassionate Healing Practice

By Peter Salomone
Shamanic Practitioner

with Robert Stephson

A Modern Shaman Speaks…

Shamanic Depossession

A Compassionate Healing Practice

By Peter Salomone

I thank the Creator for my life and for the life he has given to all of his Creation. I offer this book to Honor my Allies, my Power Animals, and my Spirit Guides. With deep reverence and respect, I am grateful for their guidance, their healing powers, their shared wisdom, and their continued friendship. I also wish to thank my Ancestors, on whose shoulders I stand, and my family for their enthusiastic and uplifting encouragement for my shamanic work. My thanks too, to Robert Stephson, for his steadfast collaboration throughout the writing of this book. Lastly, I am grateful to all my friends in the shamanic community and to all my teachers in ordinary and non-ordinary reality.

Contents

Invocation

This beloved prayer of the Sioux was translated into English in 1887 by chief Yellow Lark, the distinguished Lakota spiritual leader of the late nineteenth century.

Great Spirit Prayer

"Oh, Great Spirit, whose voice I hear in the wind,
And whose breath gives life to all the world.
Hear me! I am before you, one of your many children.
I am small and weak.
I need your strength and wisdom.
Let me walk in beauty and make my eyes
Ever behold the red and purple sunset.
Make my hands respect the things you have made,
my ears sharp to hear your voice.
Make me wise, that I might understand
the things you have taught my people.
Help me to be calm and strong
in the face of all that comes toward me.
Let me learn the lessos you have hidden in every leaf and rock.
Help me seek pure thoughts and act with the intention of helping others.
Help me find compassion, without empathy overwhelming me.
I seek strength not to be greater than my brothers,
but to be able to fight my greatest enemy − myself (with my fears and doubts).
Make me always ready to come to you
with clean hands and straight eyes,
so when life fades, like a fading sunset,
my spirit may come to you without shame.

It is my sincere hope that my audience will embark upon their individual journeys as readers with both wisdom and receptivity.

Introduction

Greetings, Dear Reader

My name is Peter Salomone, and I've written this book to help demystify a spiritual healing practice that is deeply misunderstood, of wonderful benefit, and much needed on a scale few people would suspect. I speak of depossession, which has been part of the "natural hygiene," so to speak, of countless human communities in many cultures through all time. I write this book based upon my extensive first-hand experience performing depossession for many ordinary people: the friends, family and neighbors we all know, whose sufferings have arisen from an unsuspected and widely denied cause.

To begin though, I'd like to share a bit about who I am, and how I came to practice this unusual healing art. I'd also like to clarify the terms that I use in this book, since the subject is so freighted with misconception, emotional attitudes, and unnecessary fears.

How I Became a Shamanic Healer

I lived my first thirteen years of life in Tricarico, a small town in Southern Italy whose roots are documented as far back as 849 A.D. My own family's name is documented as far back as the 15th century, so my roots are deep in this town that has a magical feel, with its still-standing architecture with Arabian, Byzantine, and Saracen influences. In my youth it was a tightly-knit community immersed in nature, tradition, and emotionality that most Americans, especially younger ones, can only imagine. Death entered my life rudely, right at the start. My father died when I was nine months old, my grandmother when I was a young boy, and my uncle, who had become a father to me, when I was eleven. These deaths in my closest family caused me much pain and suffering, to be sure. Yet they also provoked deep questions in my young mind. Quite simply, I wanted to know what was going on here, and on a big scale: the scale of life on earth, versus whatever lay beyond that.

This to-me natural questioning persisted through my adolescence and into adulthood. I moved to the United States as a teen, and later received a degree in my passion of psychology. I then took up a career in business, as seemed practical, since I had married my lady, with whom I was to raise three daughters.

Though conventional activities and pleasures occupied me for decades, the proddings of my spiritual heart were a continual under-tow, pulling from within. I did well in meeting my financial needs, but felt increasingly less successful in fulfilling my spiritual needs. In my 40's the gulf between the two became untenable. I knew that I had to champion the world as I saw it through my heart, not as I saw it through my eyes. In this sense, my story is like that of many others – perhaps your own as well – the story of embracing only later in life what one deeply values.

I remember eagerly reading Carlos Castaneda's books and feeling a strong resonance with his story. It would be years, though, before those inklings bore real fruit, when I was finally drawn to study with the father of modern core shamanism, Michael Harner, the founder of the Foundation for Shamanic Studies. I will never forget the shivers I felt in my spine the first time I was with him, sitting in a circle, when he "called in the Spirits," an invocation made at the beginning of every session working with Spirit. When in that same first session I heard celestial flute music inside myself during his invocation, I knew I had contacted a realm that was very familiar to me. I felt at home.

I know now that it is common for shamans to receive their initiation through some form of illness. Only in adulthood did I come to understand that I had myself been initiated into this calling in my childhood, not just by the deaths I have described, but by an unusual period of childhood illness. During my adolescence, for about four months I was struck by an unknown malady that had the two town doctors coming to visit me almost daily, with great concern and without success. During that time, I remember being out of my body and visiting many strange places. But I did not have the maturity to characterize these experiences, which I found quite confusing, and did not feel that I could share with others.

I studied for many years as an apprentice with Michael Harner, who came to the actual practice of shamanism via a distinguished academic career. I also worked with Alicia Luengas Gates, who came to it via a life as a Franciscan nun in Mexico, and Sandra Ingerman, who had a background in psychotherapy.

I worked with great dedication with these teachers who were profoundly versed in the mysteries of shamanism. During those years of my training, I took both core courses and many advanced courses, including practical courses on depossession, and gained much knowledge and experience.

I also underwent shamanic initiations during my training. These are specific ceremonial rituals in which one is granted a "visionary shift" by one's spirit Allies. This shift leads to an understanding of the reality of other dimensions. What one experiences during these initiations is so extraordinary that it cannot be explained by our logical mind. As a result, it spurs our mind to question the very nature of the reality we have been taught to perceive. Such initiations also lead to experiences and feats that one cannot humanly decide to "do." These initiatory experiences simply cannot be explained without acknowledging the intervention and the reality of these guiding spirits, our Allies. This dramatic shift in one's life comes to those whose destiny is to work with healing spirits to relive suffering for everything that lives. Initiation is the highest of honors given by the spirits, and it usually forces the shaman to develop humility in the face of the healing power that is shown to him or her by these Allies.

Shamanism in Our Times

There are many aspects of shamanism, and of depossession as well, that I know sound fantastical. This is particularly so in the arid, materialistic culture we live in, whose technology and mass-mentality have paved over the deeper wellsprings of human spirituality. Many older indigenous cultures, of course, knew better. They were permeated by an appreciation of the fact that there is an invisible side to life - that life is filled with mysteries and governed by laws quite different from those of human society.

While in this respect our culture may be paved over like a parking lot, many ancient and noble forms of spirituality have pushed up through the asphalt like flowers. These are not just "movements" in some abstract sense, but are real people who actually embody these traditions and their knowledge. The spirituality of such people requires not words, tradition and authority, but first-hand experience, demonstration, and transformation. My own teachers were wonderful examples of this rebirth, and increasing numbers of people are now becoming receptive to this new spirituality.

Today's shamans often teach practices that everybody can use to improve their lives. Shamanism is a very "democratic" approach to Spirit, and at the end of this book is a list of resources where you can investigate these things in more depth. In this book, though, I focus on the specific practice of depossession. Depossession involves the detachment of a spirit from a living person whose energetic field they have settled into. It is also the agreement of an intrusive spirit to vacate a place where he/she has hunkered down for reasons that, as you will see, are quite understandable, even as they may be far from innocent. In this book we will consider the dynamics that are involved in this process — which are different from those you may believe based upon religion, fable, and superstition. In this regard, I will also discuss what is commonly referred to as "exorcism." As I will show you, depossession and exorcism are entirely different — in their underlying attitudes, execution, and results. Indeed, I consider depossession to be a beneficent practice, while exorcism is not.

When it is conducted by an experienced practitioner, depossession is a positive event for all concerned. That is why I have written this book, in the hope of shedding light on the subject, purging it of fear and drama, and making this healing act both credible and congenial to a culture that rejects such things.

The Words I Use, and Why I Use Them

I'd like to define the terms I use in this book, since this will help you to understand much about how my tradition regards life, death, spirits, and depossession. Because words reflect reality so imperfectly in the things that really matter, our words should reflect, as best as possible, and our highest understanding, which are found in the depths of our heart.

Let's first consider the word "depossession." Though an imperfect term, it's about as close as we can get with a single word. I like it because it reflects the simple fact that we are "undoing" a kind of "holding" on a structural level. It is also a nicely neutral alternative to the word "exorcism." Although that word does not exclusively belong to the Catholic Church, it is commonly associated with many centuries of a specifically Catholic practice. In the film The Exorcist, it was given a lurid connotation from which it will likely never recover. This in itself is cause enough to seek a better word than exorcism.

Interestingly, while I'm o.k. with the word "depossession," I do not like the word "possessed." Having worked with a great many people who could be called "possessed," I know that there are many degrees to which they are affected. In many cases, the life of such a person has been compromised in the form of an addiction, emotional travails, health problems, or mental imbalance. And yet, in the face of such challenges they may yet lead admirable lives in terms of work, family, and service to others. There is also the other end of the spectrum, in which a person's life may be largely debased, and for all constructive purposes, destroyed. The word "possessed," though, suggests no such degrees, but only suggests the vice-like grip of slavery and loss of autonomy. This is why I use the simple words "host" and "client" to describe these human beings. As I hope you can see, I am not just picking at words here.

When it comes to the other protagonist, the invading spirit, I use a number of different terms, depending on the context: "wandering spirit," "intrusive spirit," "possessing spirit," "obsessing spirit." I also use the term "lost soul," even though it is a bit inaccurate, because most of these spirits do not know that they are lost. Terms that I not only avoid but object to, are the commonly used words "spook," "demon," "devil," "Satan" and the like. These terms are negative and abusive, and as such, are contrary to the empathetic view of my tradition. I would also note that "the devil," as commonly conceived, is a purely human invention that was created in antiquity.

The words *daemon* and *daimon* are Latinized spellings of the Greek δαίμων, which refers to the daemons of ancient Greek religion and mythology, Hellenistic religion, and philosophy. Daemons were good or benevolent "supernatural beings" who interact between mortals and gods, such as inferior divinities and the ghosts of dead heroes (see Plato's Symposium). This is quite different from the Judeo-Christian usage of the word 'demon', which intends a malignant spirit that can seduce, afflict, or possess humans. This latter usage is a myth that still serves religious authorities quite well as a means of instilling fear in people, and ascribing blame for their shortcomings and for the evils of the world. It is quite contrary to the theological idea that is far more acceptable, namely that there is nothing outside of the Creator.

In saying this, I am not suggesting that there is no such thing as evil. Our common experience tells us that there are, indeed, many things on earth and within people that can have painful, destructive, and negative effects upon us. That said, from my extensive experience and communication with lost souls, I know that above all, most of them are human spirits. While there are other, non-human entities that sometimes come into play, as well as spirits with truly bad intentions, in all cases they merit as much empathy and respect as the individual who is the "host," who we tend to regard as a victim. For in possession, as in all of nature, there is no good guy or bad guy. And if there is a victim, then there is a victim on both sides.

I refer to the person who performs the depossession as a healer, or to reflect my own experience and tradition, a shaman or shamanic healer. The word "shaman," which originates from the Tungas culture near Siberia, literally means "one who sees in the dark; one who knows." It is useful to remember that the word "shaman" is just that: a word that has persisted into contemporary times. Throughout history, depossession has also been performed by men and women who, in our language, would be called witches, warlocks, or medicine men and women - terms to which we may bring unhelpful associations. It has also been performed in all the world's major religions, which have traditionally had specialists who engage in this practice, though without achieving the sensational profile of exorcists in the Catholic Church.

What matters here is that widely differing cultures throughout history have had ways to resolve what might be called the "natural unnatural" phenomenon of possession. It is common for some people to not cross over at death, an outcome that routinely occurs as a result of sudden, accidental, or conflicted death, or a strong attachment to people or material possessions in this life. And this happens more routinely than most people think. We could say that this is "unnatural," in that it is not the ideal or norm. But Nature, of course, is full of processes that we consider "negative" or "unnatural," but which are simply the way in which nature operates.

Finally, I use a variety of words to refer to the Spirits who work with me when I perform depossession, as well as other healing practices. I use the terms Spirit, Helping Spirits, Compassionate Spirits, Spirit Allies, Power Animals, Angels and the like, depending on the context. Terminology aside, what matters most is that these Spirits are real, and the help that they offer is real. In our culture, of course, the very idea of Spirits provokes doubts and raised eyebrows, let alone the claim that one has a practical working relationship with them. Obviously, my aim here is not convince anyone of their reality, and so I leave this to the level of preparation of my reader.

The Reality of Shamanic Healing

What I share in this book is based entirely upon my first-hand experience as a shamanic healer – and I cannot emphasize this strongly enough. I say this not to suggest my own importance, but because this is essential to our emerging understanding of spiritual realities. Spiritual realities are realities that can, and must be verified: empirically, experientially, first-hand, by you, and by me. We live in an age of spiritual awakening and ferment, leaving behind the belief in an external parental Creator, and reorienting ourselves to a personal destiny in the Divinity that lives within each of us. As the old gods fall by the wayside, we come to see ourselves as human spirits who live in a multi-dimensional universe that is metaphysical as much as it is physical. And we aspire to first-hand intuition and experience of the higher dimensions that interpenetrate and interact with this one in our daily lives.

My own verifications of higher dimensions - in what shamans call "non-ordinary reality"- are not so much just "shamanic" realities, then, any more than they are Christian realities, Buddhist realities, or Hindu realities. Life is One. And whoever accesses other dimensions to contact spirit and obtain benefits for his fellow humans, is a healer - in reality. Empirical reality must be our point of reference, and healing is our confirmation of higher spiritual intervention. The benefits of depossession, as I describe it in this book, have had just such confirmation in the positive changes of my clients, and those achieved by my many colleagues. As a result of depossession, I have seen depressions lift, addictions become less severe or totally disappear, emotions stabilize, illnesses evaporate, and voices in the head disappear. A new level of psychological health, energy, and well-being is achieved. This is a wonderful reality that I hope you will better appreciate in these pages.

🦅 🦅 🦅

The rest of this book is organized as follows.

In **Chapter I**, I describe the "facts of life" regarding life, death, the after-life, and the movement of the human spirit between these two realms. Many readers will already be comfortable with the concepts I present; others perhaps less so. In any case, how we see the world has a great influence on what we consider possible, and this is particularly so in the case of spiritual healing.

In **Chapter II**, I discuss the "three-sided equation" of depossession, in which three different people interact: the host, the lost soul, and the healer. I discuss the roles that each of these people play in the process, and the different kinds of dynamics that are involved.

Chapter III presents the prelude to depossession. That is, who would profit from the process, and how people are led to find someone qualified to help them. I then discuss how one might go about choosing such a healer. I also address the subject of spiritual diagnosis, in which the shaman determines that possession is in fact the case, rather than other causes that could be the source of a person's distress.

In **Chapter IV** I describe the act of depossession itself. After discussing the setting in which it takes place, I then describe what takes place during the process: what the healer sees and does, and the dynamic interplay of the healer, the host, and the intrusive spirit – not to mention the Spirit Helpers who make it all possible.

In **Chapter V** I explain how shamanic depossession is fundamentally different from, and also antithetical to exorcism, which is the historical approach of the Catholic Church to the same basic situation.

Chapter VI is called "Aftermath – Integration." Depossession represents a breakthrough for the client and relief from a long-borne burden. It also heralds the beginning of a new phase of healing. This chapter discusses the integration that follows, as the client adjusts to a new reality. I also address the question of whether, following depossession, one can be invaded again by a wandering spirit.

Chapter VII offers a first-hand account of someone who experienced a depossession that I performed. It illuminates many aspects of the process in a real human voice.

Finally, in **Chapter VIII**, I offer a number of resources for your further consideration and study.

✦ ✦ ✦

Shamanism is a spiritual path that is available to everyone, irrespective of their religion or culture. Like myself, many shamanic practitioners teach practices that are accessible and of great benefit to everyone. Depossession, though, is not for everyone. It involves real dangers and should not be attempted by anyone who is not equipped with excellent training and experience. *Please – do not even consider making an amateur foray into this area.* I don't know how to put this any more strongly, and so will leave it at that.

✦ ✦ ✦

I wish you well on your journey through these pages. Relax, enjoy yourself, prepare to learn new things, and above all, leave your fears at the door. My wish is for depossession to be something that can harmoniously take its appropriate place in our culture and our evolving world view. And since life, in my view, is a stupendous and infinite event that invites continuous exploration, this is a subject to be approached without fear, and with an open heart.

Namaste!
Peter Salomone
Placerville, California 2014

Chapter I

Life, Death, Afterlife... and in Between

We Live in Peculiar Times

We live in peculiar times. A great many of us believe that life is a spiritual event in which our soul enters the body, leaves that body at death, then migrates to a realm where it lives on, in what most people consider to be a subtle form. Few of us, though, were raised in a religion or culture that actually gave us this belief, let alone nurtured it. Most of us adopted it intentionally in adulthood, based on study and insight that spoke directly to our hearts. And we did this in the face of a mass-culture that holds no such belief, and even negates it. I find this quite remarkable.

Most of the people who come to me for shamanic healing share this spiritual vision. In some, it's a warm hope in a newly kindled part of themselves. For others, it's a deep intuition, based on personal insight and experience. In still others, this vision of spirits leaving their physical form and crossing the threshold of the Afterlife is neither hope nor intuition, religion nor philosophy. It is a fact – a fact that they see as plainly as others see the physical world.

Life is a Healing Event

This view of ourselves as evolving citizens in an eternal cosmos has a tough side, as well. Evolution means growth, which in turn calls for personal insight, responsibility, and payment on many levels. This growth often plays out in ways we think of as healing. Indeed, we might even say that the meaning of our life on earth is to be healed, as much as any other way we might characterize it. And so – along with our newly emerging spirituality has come a wealth of insight into the ways we remain bound to a negative experience of Life. This insight has been described in terms of energy, psychology, and philosophy by countless pioneering healers.

As we become increasingly aware of the labyrinth of the psyche, we no longer blithely believe that we are all pretty much "normal." We increasingly understand that the average, "normal" person has a physical, psychic, and emotional history that can manifest in blocked, negative energies stuck in different layers of the psyche and energetic field. We find, then, a dizzying number of afflictions to which "normal" people are heir to, and an equally dizzying number of approaches to healing them.

A "New Age" that is Not so New

We might consider many of these approaches to be "New Age." But what is most striking about the "New Age" is that in many ways, it is simply the rediscovery of knowledge and techniques that have been known to many cultures in the past. It is only our naiveté that makes these discoveries seem "new," for it is an age-old understanding that the only way we can allow the Light to shine through us is via a process of healing. Even the most creative new approaches to healing typically have their roots in ancient healing practices. The cosmic vision we enjoy today is but an updated version of the vision held by others in the past. Thus, the shamanic tradition as I practice it, is but a modern version of ancient wisdom and ancient practices that have been recognized in all ages. Ultimately, we all bend the same knee that the ancients bent to the Divine, and we can all be blessed by the same Divine help that they received. If we consider the fact that Shamanism dates back about 30,000 years, we can see that shamanic practices today, and depossession specifically, are definitely not "New Age."

The Idea of Divine Help

This idea of Divine help is another idea that many of us have embraced only in our maturity. For some, it's a sweet and comforting sentiment, particularly in times of suffering or distress. For others, it's a stronger knowledge, based on extraordinary experiences that can only be explained by the presence of a Higher Hand. And finally, there are those who have developed the gift that we all have innately, of connecting and even communicating with Divine helpers - as their partners, so to speak, here on earth. This gift has been developed by men and women throughout history, just as it is being developed today by men and women on many paths, be they psychics, shamans, healers, or members of religious and spiritual orders. The Spirit is being diffused today through a wide range of channels and forms.

A genuine shamanic practitioner is one such person. As I mentioned in my introduction, I have myself undergone initiations in which I have been healed and granted alliances with Spirit Allies of various kinds. In a certain sense, they assist me in the different kinds of healing work that I do, including depossession. In a truer sense, though, I am the one who assists them. For in spiritual healing, the true healer is just a servant or channel for the Spirits coming through, who alone are able to effect the wonderful and possible healings that we pray for. In the shamanic tradition, this serving as a channel for a Higher Power is referred to as being a "hollow bone." What does "hollow" mean in this regard? It means "hollow" of judgment, pride, self-importance... of egoistic traits that impede the passage of powerful healing energies.

The experience of being a hollow bone was wonderfully described by Fools Crow, the 20th century Lakota Sioux spiritual leader and medicine man, in a conversation with Thomas E. Mails:

"... I thought about all of the stumbling blocks about me that can get in... the Helper's way when I want them to work in and through me. Then I asked them to remove these things so that I am a clean bone. They did this, and as I felt the obstacles coming out I grabbed them and threw them away. When all of this was done I felt fresh and clean. I saw myself as a hollow bone that is all shiny on the inside

and empty.... I knew then that I was ready to serve [the Helpers] well, and I held up my hand to offer my thanksgiving and to tell Him how happy I was. Immediately, I could feel the power begin to come into me, and I reached up to help it. It was wonderful, and my energy grew until I was completely filled with power. Before long I thought I would explode! Then I saw people of all races all around me, and I gave the power away to them. All of them were very grateful, and it made me feel good to share in this giving. As I emptied myself out, I could feel more power coming into me, and it was wonderful! That is how I become a little hollow tube," he said.

It was similarly described by Black Elk, the distinguished Sioux healer and medicine man whose life spanned the 19th and 20th centuries.

It was even then only after the keyota ceremony, in which I performed my dog vision, that I had the power to practice as a medicine man curing sick people; and many I cured with the power that came through me. Of course it was not I who cured. It was the power from the outer world, and the visions and ceremonies had made me like a hole through which the power could come to the two-leggeds. If I thought that I was doing it myself, the hole would close up and no power could come through. Then everything I could do would be foolish.

This is very much a partnership, then. Spirits do not have one key element of the power it takes to exercise their many healing capacities directly in ordinary reality; a "middle-man" is needed who can serve as a channel through which the power of Spirit can manifest. While Spirit is without doubt the healing power, both partners are needed equally. The physical body of the shaman serves as the vessel for Spirit's healing power, and the shaman is their ally, as a hollow bone through which they can work. I would mention, too, that the shaman never surrenders his or her own judgment as to what is needed in the process.

A shaman is one who has learned how to contact Spirits in non-ordinary reality, and through dialogue with them, is granted relationships with specific Spirits who specialize in different areas of healing.

One Spirit may work with the shaman to perform extractions, another to perform power animal or soul retrievals, and another for depossession. A good shaman thus has a number of specialists to call on.

The Reality of Disembodied Spirits Among Us

While many have an enlightened view of life, death, and the after-life, they may have a blind spot when it comes to the idea of spirits hanging around on this level. After all, since it is not a part of most people's experience, why should we consider it? Then too, the whole subject seems so dark and unpleasant! While I quite understand this attitude, it represents a definite limitation to one's spiritual understanding. Why is that? First, because it is blind to a reality that has a very real impact on many people all around us, to a degree that most people would find surprising. Indeed, it is the very commonness of spirits not crossing over, and hanging around on this level, that actually makes it an essential part of an objective spiritual world view.

How common is possession? Let me be clear. It is common, and is as much a part of life as birth and death. Although we cannot see them, spirits are everywhere, in what shaman's call the Middle World. They are able to insinuate themselves into the energetic fields of many ordinary people who we see at work, at school, in the supermarket... It may surprise you to hear that these spirits are a root cause of many addictions, illnesses, and psychological problems that afflict many "good" people like ourselves. Not to mention the many "good" people whom they may tip to "bad," that is, to the point of violence or mental imbalance. Few of us do not have family or friends who have suffered from, or continue to suffer from trials, afflictions or illnesses for which there is neither cure nor explanation. And for many of these, possession may be the root cause.

Obviously, our human family is long-suffering – as can be seen in our prisons, mental hospitals, and in the crime, war, and mischief we see on the evening news. I can tell you for a fact that possession is responsible for a significant portion of this. In Brazil, where depossession is routinely practiced by members of Spiritist churches in hospitals, psychiatric wards, prisons and private settings, they are achieving remarkable success with people suffering from schizophrenia, bipolar, addictions, and a host of pathological behaviors. Many esteemed members of the Western medical establishment are now studying this movement with direct observation, based on their intuitive regard for it. Their conclusions may never be documented in a way we will hear about on the evening news, but the scope and seriousness of their interest is in itself quite telling.

Possession, then, is a fundamental factor in human suffering, but it is not recognized as such. This is why we do well to integrate into our world view the idea of wandering souls meddling with the living. And we should do so with clarity, detachment, and compassion, so as to dispel the fear and negativity that have been cast over the subject. Only then can we appreciate the utility and blessing we are afforded by depossession. Healing is a gift of the gods, and depossession is one of these gifts, no less than modern pharmaceuticals or surgery. It is an ancient and beneficent branch of the natural healing arts.

Let us look, then, at this phenomenon of wandering souls and possession, and what this suggests in terms of the practice of depossession.

What Happens to Us at Death?

Death is a process that is as natural as the rising of the sun. We tend not to see it this way, only because we associate death with the pain that often accompanies it, and because our ego fears its extinction. I would be the last to minimize these fears, but let's agree for a moment to stand upon our highest understanding. Let's agree that just as it was the Creator's plan (or if you prefer, your soul's plan) for all of us to come here, so it was also the Creator's 's plan for us to leave one day – just as it has been for all people for all time. What, then, would be the natural playing out of this process of death?

Imagine a biblical scene in a painting by Rembrandt... a patriarch lies dying in his bed in his home, surrounded by friends and fam-

ily. His affairs are in order, and the moment of his departure is anticipated with religious feeling by all concerned. What would the word
"religious" mean, in this context? For the dying man it would mean
acceptance, a positive attitude, a profound anticipation of the transition taking place, and the expectancy of good, once he has departed.
For those close to him, it would mean all of this as well - along with
a heightened appreciation of the life to be continued, without him,
temporarily, here on earth.

What happens then, when the patriarch finally dies? In fact: all of
the good that was anticipated! For as shamans know from first-hand
perception, death is definitely an event of "crossing." And they likewise know that Compassionate Spirits are in attendance to personally
help each person move through the threshold between this world and
the next. And while this crossing has a grand and mystical aspect, it is
also as definite and natural as bringing your children to school in the
morning, seeing them greeted by their teachers on the school steps,
then watching them disappear together through the school doors. It is
this passage through this threshold that most basically constitutes death.

Unfortunately, life is not always a Rembrandt painting, and for
many, that death is neither peaceful nor embraced with understanding.
The circumstances of one's death may well determine how we navigate our passage from this plane. How easy it is to catalogue the many
ways in which death can "go wrong." People die suddenly, or violently, from strokes, from heart attacks, in plane crashes, car accidents,
crimes and wars. People die gripped by terrible fear, or with tremendous resistance, or with powerful unresolved conflicts and unfulfilled
desires. When this is the case – and unfortunately, it is often the case
– the person's spirit does not cross over into the next realm. The spirit
has left its body, but it remains hovering, in a subtle form that is visible to shamans in the Middle World of non-ordinary reality, which
coincides with the very physical environments that you and I live in.
There, it continues to exist, every bit as real as the equally invisible
oxygen, microbes, and humidity we all believe in.

What do these shocked, confused and hovering spirits often do?
They do what any person would do who finds himself thrust into a
sudden, shocking homelessness. They look for the nearest shelter. The
spirit may thus eventually insinuate itself into the energy field of liter-

ally anybody who is vulnerable and conveniently at hand. And there it finds a new home, a safe haven that offers some degree of the energy and comfort of a human body living a human life. Paradoxically, while we might regard these spirits as heavy and "earth-bound," they are in some ways subtler and "lighter" than we are – we, whose energy fields remain tethered to a physical body. Because these spirits consist only of "spirit," they have the capacity to invade another person's energy field and perform the seemingly "magical" act of possession.

The strangest part of this - which many people find hard to grasp – is that this event of possession, in our culture, is often hardly an intentional act, let alone a malevolent act. Indeed, this spirit typically has no real grasp of what has happened, and may not even realize that it has died. This is why we need to make some adjustments in our thinking. First, we need to accept the idea that possession is a fairly common event. And second, we need to divest this event of all the negative associations we have with it. In the shamanic view, it is a common human situation that calls for a practical, compassionate response. This is why shamans consider depossession to be an act of spiritual hygiene.

As I suggested earlier, it is also true that there are intrusive spirits who do enter another person intentionally, a subject we will address later in a number of contexts.

What Happens Next?

Once two entities are sharing a single body, we then have two "roommates" living in a room that was intended for only one. A nice overview of what then takes place in possession was given in an interview with the distinguished contemporary shaman, Betsy Bergstrom.

> *"When possession occurs, the effect on the living person may vary greatly. Often, the feeling is one of being what I call 'overshadowed'. The emotional state of the deceased, as well as their fears, predilections, vices, desires and even bodily locations of illness, injury or trau-*

ma may be transferred to the living host... a sort of fusing of two people with only one body between them... such that neither person will really do well with the situation. A possessing spirit may be able to experience some of what the living host is feeling, ingesting, or doing, but it will always be muffled and unsatisfactory... The possessing spirit may push harder to get their desires met, even driving the host to death, but never truly satisfying their desires because of the inherent piggy-backing nature of the connection... The average possession or overshadowing can result in illness, anger, fear, depression, mood swings, voices in the head, experiencing what seems like a past life, nightmares, and sexual stimulation."

As you can see, Betsy's description suggests a wide range of possible dynamics for this new, unconscious "partnership" that has arisen. In the next chapter, I will describe how this plays out in more detail. My point here is that the host is now continually subject to a phantom human influence that they do not understand, and it can compromise their independence, health, well-being, and even survival in many and different ways.

How Can We Know This is True?

To the practiced inner eye of a shaman, the presence of disembodied spirits in the Middle World, hovering in our environment, and insinuated within their human hosts, is a reality that is as apparent as "the nose on your face." How, though, can a person who does not have such vision, accept that this is actually true? In many cultures throughout history, the question never arises. Possession and depossession is accepted as a fact of life. Not only has it been enshrined in these older cultures' oral teachings, religious rites, arts, and lore, but its reality is continually borne out in practice, and proved by the practical results obtained. This is what gives these traditions such enduring vitality. What appears to the skeptical modern eye as superstitious, as needing proof, to the earth-wise traditions is simple fact.

Our modern culture has lost the thread of such traditions. To help people pick up the thread again, I like to share the following analogy. When the dentist takes x-rays of our teeth, we cannot see the x-rays. We trust, however, in the insight and experience of the physicists who learned to produce and manipulate x-rays, and in the dentists who use them. If we have any doubt as to whether x-rays actually exist, it is put to rest when we see the images that are produced by that invisible process, which show dark spots on exactly the tooth surface where we feel pain.

Likewise, any doubt we might have about the reality of possessing spirits can be put to rest by the results that modern healers are achieving for their clients. Whether it be the end of an addiction, a vice, a pain, distress, voices in the head… the proof is experienced by the client, and in turn, by those around him or her. In my own practice, and the practice of my colleagues, the truth of possessing spirits, of depossession, and of the healing that follows it, has been proven many thousands of times. In many societies this proof has been repeated for so many centuries and become so enshrined in tradition that no one would even think to doubt it. Only because today's scientific culture has become so divorced from such wisdom and practices, does the idea of "proof" become an issue. Clearly we have a need for re-education in the ways of the spirit world.

Chapter II

A Three-sided Human Equation

In this chapter we look at the three-sided equation that constitutes a shamanic depossession. They are, of course: (1) the person who has unknowingly become the host to an intrusive spirit, (2) the intrusive spirit, and (3) the healer, whose aim is to free the client from their uninvited guest, and to enable the spirit to move on and make a transition from the earth plane.

As regards the host, the most common questions I am asked are: Who gets invaded by a wandering spirit, and how were they vulnerable to this? Why one person rather than another? Are there certain circumstances that are conducive to possession? How can one protect oneself against it? (I discuss the symptoms of possession in Chapter 3.)

As regards the intrusive spirit, the most common questions are: Who are these spirits? Why do they invade other people? What do they get out of it, and how do they get it? What are the dynamics of the life they share with their host?

And finally, as regards the shaman: Who becomes such a healer? How do they learn to perform depossession? How does this fit in with our Western religious and cultural traditions and beliefs?

Let's look, then, at these three sides of the equation, so we can better understand the dynamics of the process.

The Host

Who Gets Invaded, and Why?

People who have a strong, sound spiritual energy field are not invaded by wandering spirits. Their spiritual strength (which is different from physical strength) naturally repels such a possibility. Possession occurs to individuals who are suffering from a significant degree of what shamans call "power loss." As the terms implies, power loss is a kind of debilitation that is commonly experienced in many ways: through illness, trauma, accidents, psychological shocks, and unresolved conflicts of all kinds. Though most people are not aware that they have guardian spirits, such as power animals, in fact they do – much to their benefit. However, through the commission of bad acts, such as inflicting pain upon others, people may be abandoned by their guardian spirits, which then leaves them vulnerable to intrusive spirits. Thus, power loss can be experienced by anyone at any age, regardless of their apparent physical strength, and despite seemingly positive appearances.

Soul loss is a precursor to power loss – which must be intentionally restored. Since there are different degrees of soul loss, there are different degrees and kinds of afflictions to which one becomes vulnerable.

We've all seen enough science fiction movies to be able to visualize how power loss would deplete the energy field of an individual. A shamanic healer, though, is able to actually see a depleted energy field, in terms of energy holes, blockages, leaks, patterns, and the like. As a general understanding, though, it is enough to know that power loss is basically a feeling of weakness and emptiness, as opposed to fullness and strength. It is a debilitating factor that diminishes one's constructive capacities.

Though people commonly translate the idea of "power loss" into "energy loss," the term "power loss" better communicates the shamanic view that we are each endowed by the Creator with the power to realize our potentiality – to fully express our destiny. This power is the birthright and hallmark of a healthy person. When trauma has caused parts of our soul to leave us, a vacuum is created. This vacuum may be large or small, depending upon the amount of soul loss. While one person may have the resilience to bounce back from a terrible accident with no power loss, another may experience significant loss from a relatively minor accident or negative experience. Clearly, then, there's no sense in enumerating the many situations that engender power loss, and seeking some kind of correspondence between power loss and certain kinds of affliction. The essential point is whether or not there is power loss, and the vulnerability that accompanies it.

The Shamanic Model of Illness and Healing

Power loss can manifest in three distinct **modes** of affliction, which shamans describe as **intrusions**, **soul loss**, and **possession**. Though these three afflictions have a common origin in power loss, they are not three different degrees of the same thing. I'd like to briefly discuss intrusions and soul loss because they give us an essential context in which to understand possession. And to understand them in their proper context, we must first understand the shamanic model of healing, which is quite different from the medical and psychological models we have been brought up to believe in.

In the conventional view, physical maladies exist only if they can be seen, or measured by instruments. As for psychological afflictions, they are considered to be a kind of indeterminate "something" that may lie in our biochemistry, in our brain synapses, or in some nebulous place we vaguely refer to as "the mind" or "psyche." Unless drugs are prescribed, the question of where our problems actually reside does not even arise in treatment; it is considered too theoretical.

Shamans, however, know that many afflictions have a quite definite origin that also has a definite location where they can be intentionally accessed for our benefit. They exist in a spiritual form in what shamans call "non-ordinary" reality, which is very much "off the radar screen" of Western medicine – and Eastern medicine as well, despite its recognition of subtle energies. A shaman's gift lies in knowing the laws that govern these spiritual forms, and in being able to access them in the service of healing. Let us look first, then, at intrusions, and then at soul loss, before we come to our subject of possession. As you will see, the picture that they draw is quite different from reality as we normally consider it.

Intrusions ‑ Extraction

Intrusions are non-human entities in non-ordinary reality that can enter the holes in a person's energy field that are caused by soul loss. Once nestled inside a person, they can cause afflictions of many kinds, ranging from aches and pains, to fevers and flu. And if the soul loss is great enough, the door can be opened to more degenerative conditions and full-blown disease. Non-ordinary reality is a subtle metaphysical reality that is coincident with the ordinary world that we live in. It is the home of a wide range of subtle entities and energies, which include the forms of uncongenial creatures that we all know, such as wasps and spiders, as well as a host of other unfamiliar life forms. Have you ever seen photos from the depths of the ocean, in which all sorts of strange life forms are adrift in a kind of "soup" of organic life? This is a good metaphor for what exists in non-ordinary reality, hidden from our sight.

Interestingly, we have accepted the view of modern science that we are surrounded by invisible germs, microbes, and gaseous elements that affect us, but we have yet to accept shamanism's 30,000 years of verification that we are also surrounded by these other kinds of entities. In an objective sense, when these entities enter a human being, they are simply flowing into a promising new location. Like all of nature, they live opportunistically, and gravitate toward environments that will best support them. It's only because they don't belong in a human being that we call them intrusions. The degree of a person's power loss determines the number and degree of intrusions to which they may be vulnerable. One of the basic skills of a shamanic healer is the discovery and the subsequent extraction of these intrusions.

As we mentioned earlier, there are degrees of possible intrusions.

These can range from entities as small as a gnat, an insect, a nail, or a rock, to substances of various natures whose chemistry simply does not belong inside a human body. Once they have entered the human body, these different kinds of intrusions may then undergo different degrees of development.

It is outside the scope of this book to explain intrusions and extraction in detail, but a brief sketch will be helpful, particularly in order to better understand possession. A client came to me complaining of a persistent cough. She had also noted a new and peculiar weight gain around her lower belly. With shamanic vision (which I explain in Chapter 4) I could see that a pool of dark "gunk" had gathered in her lower belly, and that it formed a kind of cord that led up to her throat. I extracted the gunk and the cord, and disposed of them in water. The woman's cough disappeared, and over time, her weight gain melted away, as well.

Eastern or Western medical doctors could have approached my client's problem from any number of perspectives, and could have offered any number of palliative measures. It is quite unlikely, though, that they would have directly linked her throat with her belly. And they certainly would not have directly disposed of the pathological material that was the true origin of these two symptoms. My point is by no means to indicate the superiority of shamanic healing over other healing arts. Rather, it is to suggest that there are maladies for which shamanic healing is best able to produce effective results.

Let's look next at soul retrieval, which is a kind of reverse process, in which something that should be **inside** a person, is stuck **outside of** them.

Soul Retrieval

Trauma is our common human heritage. When a person experiences a physical, emotional or psychological shock that is more than they can bear, a portion of their soul leaves their body. Modern psychology has helped us to understand this idea of split-off or dissociated parts of ourselves, and most people can readily and intuitively accept this idea. These split-off "soul parts" compromise our integrity, and like wounds, can affect us in many ways. There is an important part of this picture, though, that modern psychology does not grasp at all. It is the fact that these parts have split off in a very literal, concrete sense, and that they continue to exist in a very definite place in non-ordinary reality. There, they are preserved in a visible form that has a definite location, a distinct presence, and specific content that is associated with why they left. Most importantly of all, the energy that fled the person lies waiting to be recovered.

By journeying to non-ordinary reality, an experienced shaman is able to locate and communicate with this split-off part, bring it back to ordinary reality, and literally infuse it back into the person. This constitutes nothing less than the reintegration of the soul part and the vital energy that modern psychology concedes has been lost, but only hopes that the client may one day recover as a result of insight, dream-work, and therapy.

The shamanic process of soul retrieval, also quite differently, involves no prolonged discussion, no fishing for clues from the past, and it does not take place over a lengthy period of time. It is a specific healing event, a spiritual intervention, in which soul parts are straightforwardly recovered for a person. To be sure, there is a process of integration that follows soul retrieval, and this involves healing that does take place over time. But what is remarkable and different about soul retrieval is that a breakthrough of real significance takes place in a single healing event.

At a workshop I performed a soul retrieval for a woman whose physique should have made her quite an imposing figure. Her shoulders were strongly bowed forward, though, and mirroring this, her entire self-presentation was "caved in." Journeying to non-ordinary reality, I was able to see that she had undergone a very unfortunate experience, which from that point forward had affected both her posture and psychology. With the help of Spirit, I was able to infuse her with the energy that had fled from her (thus returning her lost soul parts), and restore her energetic integrity. Some shamans will share with the client the "story" of the event which created the event of soul loss, which could be anything from a rape to a divorce to a physical accident. Others, like myself, prefer instead to offer a "healing story" that does not look back, but that will inspire the person to reclaim their lost integrity following the soul retrieval. Still others dispense with the story of the soul loss as well as the healing story, feeling that the return of the lost soul part or parts will in itself bring about the desired healing.

In any event, the return of the lost energy is apparent, to both the client and the healer. In this instance, I could immediately see a new vitality coursing through this woman, which would enable her to reclaim both the posture and self-worth she had lost. It was already visible in her stance and in the spark in her eye. She was aware of this as well, and while her understanding of what she had recovered would deepen in the days to come, she knew that something of great significance had taken place, for which she was greatly appreciative.

Obviously, soul retrieval, like intrusions and extraction, is a subject that merits more attention than I can offer here. I would recommend the book 'Soul Retrieval', by Sandra Ingerman, as an excellent source for learning more. For the purposes of our present discussion, though, I would also like to mention two other key ideas. The first is that the shaman's remarkable ability to locate and retrieve the split-off parts of a person's soul is entirely dependent upon the wisdom and participation of the shaman's Spirit Allies. The shaman, remember, is a "hollow bone," a trained intermediary between physical reality and the spiritual reality that penetrates and influences it. The second idea is that the client's acceptance of the reality of subtle dimensions and the beneficent assistance of Spirit is instrumental in arriving at a healing outcome.

Possession

I have taken this little detour on soul retrieval and intrusions in order to impress upon you (without fear) our potential vulnerability to invasion by unseen forces, and to the outward flight of soul parts due to trauma. Neither of these is acknowledged by medical science, nor are they adequately addressed by our common psychological or religious frameworks. I hope I have also helped you to appreciate the ability of shamanic healing to deal with such problems.

The vulnerability that accompanies power loss, then, has degrees, which brings us back to our subject at hand. At the far end of the spectrum, when a person's power loss is great enough, it becomes possible for the wandering spirit of a dead human being to invade them. Our energetic system, our bodies, and indeed, our very lives themselves, provide a medium that is a "perfect fit" for such a spirit. As you can see, then, a person who comes to a shaman for healing may be manifesting a problem, or problems, that have three possible origins: a split-off part of the soul that can be recovered via soul retrieval, one or more intrusions, or possession. Because all three of these are related to different kinds and degrees of soul loss, it is entirely possible for a person to be suffering from two or even all three of these. This of course raises the important subject of spiritual diagnosis, which I address in detail in the next chapter.

Why One Person and Not Another?

As I mentioned earlier, possession takes place quite randomly among people due to their power loss. It is also possible, though less common, for the spirit of a dead person to "shadow" someone to whom they felt a strong attachment while in life. This "shadowing" may take place if a person does not have power loss sufficient for the wandering spirit to fully insinuate itself into their energy field, but still has a degree of vulnerability. In this kind of event, which is short of complete invasion, the obsessing spirit may linger and harass the person to differing degrees. We refer to this kind of 'shadowing' as "attachment."

To give an example of this... A client came to me who was experiencing great distress. During her adolescence, her uncle wanted to abuse her sexually, and made an attempt to do so, albeit unsuccessfully. Some time later he died, but he continued to appear to her in dreams that she found disturbing. What is noteworthy here is that modern psychology would ascribe her dreams only to the recycling and elaboration of her memories - not to the present interference of the spirit of a dead person. A shaman, though, knows that there are other possibilities, and that though this may lead to some "dark places," there is also the promise of real resolution.

For this woman I performed a process quite similar to the process of depossession that I describe in detail in Chapter 4. Though her uncle was not actually within her energy field, he was nonetheless trapped in non-ordinary reality, and could therefore be persuaded that a much better destiny was available to him. And with the help of the Compassionate Spirits, I was able to guide him in his passage to the Other Side, thus relieving my client of her distress.

Full possession, though, most commonly takes place in a way that is quite simple, and once you grasp it, also quite understandable. The lost soul who is drifting in confusion simply "ducks in" to whatever nearby human being happens to present an energy system that is vulnerable – i.e., a person with significant soul loss. Although there are, in fact, predators in the Middle World who know quite well what they are doing, often there is no deliberation involved, and none of the predation or psychological profiling that we might imagine. We might liken such a lost soul to a person caught in a storm who opens the first door that he finds unlocked. This being the case, there is often nothing intentional about the wandering soul's selection of its host - and likewise, no particular reason why the host attracts a particular spirit to it. If you recall the analogy I gave earlier, the entire event is rather impersonal, like the flowing of water from one place to another.

This is often, but not always the case, though. As I suggested earlier, there is also the scenario in which a downright predatory spirit intentionally preys upon people in order to enslave and subjugate them. Such a spirit may even make a "career" of this, inhabiting one person until they die, then jumping into another, lifetime after lifetime, in serial fashion. Though a spirit of this kind can certainly be a "tougher nut to crack" for the shaman, they too will usually yield to a skilled practitioner. The reason for this, which we will explore in more depth later, is the essential humanity of these spirits. Despite the seeming success of their control and domination, and the "rewards" they seem to enjoy, they are essentially stuck and dissatisfied. Possession does not truly relieve the unresolved conflict that kept them here in the first place. Thus, they are victims of their own character defects, and as such - appearances to the contrary - are by no means in the driver's seat.

There is a third case that deserves brief mention here, as well. Not all spirits who inhabit the Middle World of non-ordinary reality after death are confused, traumatized, or have bad intentions. In certain cultures, the souls of some people who have died return to the Middle World in order to serve as custodians of ancestral lands or holy places, or protectors of their lineage. These souls might be considered to be quasi-compassionate spirits, for while they selflessly perform a beneficial service for their people, they will attack those who violate them or their lands, and do so in a highly selfish and even violent manner. This is quite different from the Spirits a shaman works with, whose purity and intention is high above the fray of human vengeance and selfishness.

What Circumstances Favor Possession? How Can One Protect Oneself?

As we have seen, there are realms that co-exist with the physical world we are all familiar with, which shamans call non-ordinary reality. And in these realms, lost spirits are wandering pretty much everywhere. But, just as we don't see the cross-fire of wi-fi beams when we walk into Starbucks, we don't see the wandering spirits who are drifting about around us. Following their deaths, after which they did not leave the Middle World, these lost souls tend to wander in the general geographical area where they died. In places where there have been wars and calamities, and places where there is a greater prevalence of death, such as hospitals and cemeteries, there is a greater concentration of wandering souls.

In northern California, where I live, there are numerous wandering spirits of Native Americans who were killed in the name of Manifest Destiny. In Europe, where there was an unprecedented scale of mass carnage in two wars, there are concentrations that are many times greater. I find it remarkable that our society knows about concentrations of plastics in remote parts of the Pacific Ocean, and about the congestion in outer space caused by dead satellites in eternal orbit, yet we remain blind to the congestion of the very space we live in by disincarnate entities. Truly, our culture and our destructive ways are causing a "population explosion" in the Middle World of non-ordinary reality, and this is not at all good for the hygiene of the living. Ancient cultures addressed the deaths of their people in order to make sure that the recently dead crossed over. They had traditions, rituals, and shamanic practices that made sure of it. Our present culture has no such knowledge, though. And as in so many areas, it simply aggravates the problem with its denial.

Is there something we should be doing, then, to protect ourselves from possible invasion by lost souls? Yes, but it has nothing to do with magic amulets or hopeful prayers. The only true protection comes from being power-filled on an energetic level. This doesn't mean that we need to become some kind of superman or superwoman brimming with special energy. Rather, it means that we need to maintain a robust connection with Spirit in order to maintain a psychological and physical integrity and well-being that results in our being power-filled. There are a great many physical, psychological, religious and spiritual practices that people pursue to keep themselves centered, in balance, and strong in every way. And I have great respect for all of these.

From the shamanic perspective, though, there are distinct practices that are specifically designed to address the kind of vulnerability we are speaking about here. These basically involve forging a connection with the spirit world by learning shamanic journeying, forging a relationship with allies and power animals, and getting shamanic healing when it is called for. While other practices may serve one well in many ways, they are not necessarily adequate in this specific sense. The dynamics of the various potentially negative forces in the Middle World of non-ordinary reality are specific and verifiable. The hygienic practices one can follow to stay healthy are likewise specific and verifiable. That said, even in shamanic practices, one must steer clear of superstition, empty ritual, and mere wishful hopes. We will speak of this topic further in Chapter 6.

The Wandering Souls

Who Are These People?

In many indigenous cultures there were rituals and practices which one could follow in order to prepare for death via the intentional experience of non-ordinary reality. In our own culture, of course, we have no such preparation - not to mention the great silence and denial that surround the transition we call death. Because wandering souls have usually experienced sudden, accidental, or tragic deaths for which they were quite unprepared, they include people of all social classes, religions, levels of education, and culture – the full range of human diversity. They may also be people with varying degrees of what we would call normalcy. And they may also possess character traits that we would call abnormal, or vices. On the furthest end of the spectrum, possessing spirits may possess traits that are downright undesirable and extreme, crossing the line into psychopathology or criminality. In short, a possessing spirit could be just about anybody.

Given that they represent such a cross-section of *humanity*, we really need to stop conceiving of possessing spirits as evil, negative, demonic, etc. That said, I do not want to sugar-coat the matter for my reader, for there are also many downright unsavory and ill-intentioned spirits out there, and the effects of their possession may well seem to justify this judgment. But as I emphasize throughout this book, the wandering soul is just that: a human soul. And in the view of my tradition, a human soul – any soul – deserves to be regarded with dignity and compassion. For this person, whoever they may be, deserves every possibility of further development and progress along the High Road of Life.

Let us put aside, too, the notion that they are strong and masterful figures. Typically they are anything but this, and usually quite the contrary. These may be people who died under anesthesia and have muddled thinking. Or pathetic figures who were overwhelmed by their circumstances. Or people shocked by traumas that were beyond their capacity to process. What these souls have in common is that they are human, they are lost, and they need help.

It is this feeling that inspires the shaman in his work, whose goal is simply to bring the help that is needed. While the **call** for help comes to me from the host, I consider it equally an opportunity to offer help to the lost soul, if he or she will permit it. True, this lost soul has not exactly requested my help. And when presented with my offer of help, they may even show great resistance or intransigence.

Based on my experience, though, and the experience of my many colleagues, these lost souls can typically be helped to move on, and most importantly, they do so of their own free will, after having been convinced by a shaman. When I see a lost soul being helped across the threshold by Compassionate Spirits, I know that I have done right not just by my client, but for that lost soul as well. Strange to say, one of the biggest differences between the host and the intrusive spirit may only be that the host may have had a clearer view that something was wrong and needed to be fixed.

What Do Wandering Souls Get from Possession?

What do they get out of it? Let's try to imagine, if we can, the situation of such a person. Imagine that one moment you were reading this book, then the next moment you were disembodied, and did not know what had happened. Of course, we can't *really* imagine this, but we can try to appreciate the fact that lost souls have suffered an inconceivable shock, are adrift and confused – and do not even know they are dead.

The main thing that is offered to such people by a living person with power loss is that person's energy and experience. Insinuated in that person's body, the lost soul can again feel things, taste foods, see the world, and vicariously participate in the host's life. They can also influence that person's life by expressing their own thoughts, feelings, and tendencies of every kind. The host offers a comfortable haven in which they can have a familiar experience of human life, which seems far better than the disembodied state they were experiencing previously.

That said, theirs is a dim and muted version of the host's experience, with none of the keenness, intelligence, and choice experienced by a living person with integrity. Theirs is a darkened world without past or future, without reflection, without aspiration, without friends. And since they are having a clouded experience of what is essentially an unnatural situation, it is inherently unsatisfactory. This is a crucial point, for as we shall see in the next chapter, it is precisely this inherently unsatisfactory quality of their experience that enables the shaman to succeed in helping them move on.

As you might guess from the happenstance nature of possession, the match-up between the character of the host and the character of the lost soul is open to endless variety. A host may be inhabited by a possessing soul with traits that are strongly contradictory to their own, mildly contradictory, or anywhere in between. These will of course produce very different kinds of dynamics and experience. A host may even be invaded by a lost soul who has a relatively passive character, and is content to sit quietly in the background, so to speak. That said, even such a mild possessing spirit is actively feeding upon the host's energy field, which is a fairly devastating event in and of itself.

The Healer

What Is a Shamanic Healer?

A shamanic healer is a person with an extraordinary gift who has developed that gift in order to be of healing service to the community. In indigenous cultures, the role of shaman was, and is, an intrinsic part of community life, and depossession is often just one of a shaman's many skills. With their trained ability to navigate in non-ordinary reality, a shaman is able to interact with the various forces that live there, and operate safely with intelligence, intentionality, and good will. Above all, the shaman forms alliances with a variety of powerful spiritual sources with whom he or she is able to work cooperatively.

At the mere mention of dealing with invisible spirits, our minds may summon forth a variety of images and associations that are negative, exaggerated, and even frightening. I would really urge you to dispel these associations. In most cases they have been suggested to us by writers and film-makers whose only goal is to manufacture and exploit their sensational products. They have nothing to do with the beneficent healing that I have seen and that my clients have experienced, or with the healing that my many colleagues and their many clients have experienced.

Who Becomes a Shamanic Healer?

Who has the gift of becoming a shamanic healer? We all have different gifts that are given to us by the Creator, as part of the Divinity found in all of us. What matters is that the gift is honored, and given the training and experience it needs in order to bear good fruit. Just as a person with a strong musical talent must study and practice in order to bring delight to many listeners, so too with a shaman. The gift makes itself known inside a person, and like a musician, the shaman must then find the teachers and circumstances that can help him or her develop this gift, this calling.

Shamanism is thus a kind of natural priesthood, a calling, a vocation that assumes different forms, depending upon the culture. In indigenous societies this training may take place in a cave, a tent, or a forest. In the West, it may take place in a home, a meeting hall, or a private office. No matter what the epoch or culture, what matters is the authenticity of the training, which entirely depends upon the authenticity of the connection that is forged between the healer and Spirit.

In Carlos Castaneda and some other books, the shaman is portrayed as an outsider, a rogue, an inspired "crazy." While I have no doubt that such characters exist, in the West, and particularly in my own tradition, the healer is typically an ordinary person who has met the challenges of career and family life in our modern Western culture. We conform to the forms and conventions of decent society, even as our work is definitely on the fringe of conventional understanding and acceptance. This is one reason why today's shaman's often call themselves "shamanic practitioners," in a concession to the kind of terminology that is acceptable in American culture. It is also true that no degree or certification confers the status of shaman upon one. A shaman is called to this vocation by Spirit, in a relationship that necessarily involves deep humility on the part of the healer. That person's recognition as being a shaman, then, can never be the result of self-promotion, but rather, is the result of recognition by the community that he or she serves. In this regard, Michael Harner offers the following straightforward remark. "People ask me, 'How do you know if somebody's a shaman'. I say, 'It's simple. Do they journey to other worlds? And do they perform miracles?" Only if the power of Spirit is coming through a person will such healings take place, and is that person recognizable as a shaman.

I would also note here, that as shamanic practice has begun to flower in our contemporary culture, a commonly held attitude has arisen that considers indigenous shamanic healers to be more genuine, or even more effective, than those who were born to a non-traditional circumstance. To be sure, I understand and share the deep respect that is due to indigenous healers, who have often maintained their "old ways" in the face of difficult challenges. I also understand how such an attitude might arise, given that non-indigenous healers often adopt some of the outward forms of traditional ways.

That said, indigenous healers have no intrinsic superiority simply due to their cultural background. The Compassionate Spirits in non-ordinary reality are of a celestial nature that transcends time, place, and culture. The alliances they form with humans, and the gifts that they offer, are not distributed on the basis of race, culture, or background. As we move into the new era that is before us, we need to recognize that true spiritual healers draw from a common spiritual source, so there is no sense in imposing our all-too-human tendency to compare and see differences among them.

Who Heals?

A ny true shamanic healer will be quick to tell you that it is not they, but the Compassionate Spirits that work through them, who are the healers. This is also true in the case of possessing souls, who are at times helped to pass to the next level by Compassionate Spirits, who stand in attendance in order to facilitate their passage to the Other Side. The person who is being healed plays a significant role as well, for their courage, intuition, and soul-desire are important elements in their healing. And for the integration that follows depossession, a person's own inner resources, which lie in the mysterious depths of our being – are also significant factors. It is an inexplicable and wonderful fact that a shaman can be a channel through which our own inner revelation may be conducted to us.

To be fair, though, I must also say that a true shaman is very much an agent of healing, as well. By tapping into advice received from spirit guides, a shaman can become a skilled diagnostician of the spiritual cause of diseases in realms that many of us may sense or intuit, but do not know how to see, navigate, or employ to our benefit. Working with the tools of their hands, voice, and sound (drums, rattles, and bells), a shaman is able to manifest healing power that emanates from his or her Allies with great immediacy and power, in ways people may find startling. And these more technical skills are strongly wedded to an insight into human psychology, and to a human heart, that are both developed to a high degree.

"Tools of the Trade"

I am myself a shamanic practitioner who was trained in the tradition of 'Core Shamanism'. Core shamanism is a movement within the modern resurgence of shamanism, which was founded by Michael Harner and has now achieved world-wide stature and recognition. Combining his personal shamanic initiations and experience with rigorous study of shamanic traditions worldwide, Harner sought to identify the basic essentials of shamanic practice that were common to all traditions, shorn of their different cultural and religious trappings. The result was a body of knowledge that made the practice of shamanism both accessible and acceptable to men and women in the West. It also gave birth to a lineage of teachers who have been granted genuine alliances with Helping Spirits.

In this new tradition, certain ancient tools are used that have also been used in ages past. As in my work, this involves the use of drums, rattles, bells, and the burning of herbs such as sage, cedar, and sweet grass. These are used as part of rituals that create an appropriate atmosphere, to help in the clearing of stuck or negative energies, and that foster a connection with the sacred. These various rituals also directly impact the energy field of the client and of the healer as well.

Take, for example, the use of drums, rattles, and bells. Modern science tells us that the rhythmic beat of a drum or rattle, as employed by indigenous healers worldwide (ranging from 3 to 4.5 beats per second), creates Theta waves in our brain activity. This induces what is called a Theta state, in which it becomes possible to receive intuitive insights of many kinds that are hidden from us in our usual Alpha and Beta states. Researchers have verified that the Theta state can increase our creativity, enhance learning, reduce stress, and also awaken our intuition and extrasensory perception.

In shamanism, the Theta state is produced by sonic percussion, and is then used to facilitate what is called "journeying," which is the exploration of non-ordinary reality. A shaman is a person who is experienced at navigating and acting in non-ordinary reality, which is where the Compassionate Spirits reside, and where the healing process largely takes place.

Shamans worldwide also use prayers and invocations. These are uttered words (which of course reflect unuttered intentions and feelings) that articulate our hopes for the healing, and our respect for the Compassionate Spirits we are inviting to participate. I invite my clients to share in these invocations, whether aloud or in silent assent, in order that we may be aligned in our feeling and aspiration. Prayer is a many-sided subject, and there are many who doubt the efficacy of prayer. In the case of experienced shamans who have a working relationship with Spirit, the main thing I would say regarding this aspect, is that their prayers get answered! The healings that are produced are also the tangible results of their prayers. And it is this that gives shamanic healing its mystical quality, even though it is not a religion per se, and takes a form quite different from the religions we are familiar with.

My overall aim, then, is to create a setting that is pleasing to the Spirits, congenial to my clients, and conducive to healing. While this setting may look strange to the modern eye, I would suggest that this is only because the modern eye has been blinded. Our culture knows only the practice of physical healing, which is done in an antiseptic room, preferably with stainless steel tables, by someone wearing a starched white jacket, and maybe a surgical mask to protect them from our germs. We are not yet used to the idea of spiritual healing, which is just as real, and has very different requirements.

In the different shamanic traditions, ritually created atmosphere, an appeal to the sacred, and purity of intent are all part of the healing process. To this end, the healer may wear symbolic clothes and arti-facts, as we see in the garb and head dresses of the Native Americans, and in the animal-spirit costumes of other shamanic cultures world-wide. In modern shamanism in the West, we dress as we see fit. Some practitioners like to wear elements of ceremonial garb drawn from different traditions, as suits their sensibility and aesthetics. Others sim-ply wear what is comfortable. In my own case, with the exception of special ceremonies, this often means jeans and a T-shirt.

Shamanic Vision and Navigation in Non-ordinary Reality

Shamans are able to work in non-ordinary reality, or the sha-manic state of consciousness, because they have a developed capacity for shamanic perception, which is also called "seeing from the heart." Shamans know that the heart is not just a pump or a muscle; it is also an organ of perception. I would like to describe to you how this sha-manic perception takes place.

Each of us is able to function in the physical world because we can see the people, creatures, and objects in it, and because we have the mental and physical capacities to influence and communicate with them. In much the same way a shaman is equipped with a trained capacity to "see" in non-ordinary reality, and to communicate and perform a variety of actions in these realms. I put the word "see" in quotation marks, because there are ways of seeing other than through our eyes.

Have you ever seen Kirilian photography, which shows the auras of physical objects as colors? In Kirilian photos of human beings, it can be seen that the energy of the body can far exceed the boundaries of the physical body. Such photos offer concrete corroboration of the reality of the human energy field. Being attuned to that dimension, a shaman is able to directly perceive the energy fields of other people and of spiritual entities in the environment. This immediate mode of perception consists of information that is transmitted on a completely different "channel" from the impressions we receive from our five senses.

When we see another person, we are largely struck by their body, their movements, their face, their clothes, their voice, and the words they say. From the viewpoint of shamanic perception, all of this is a distraction.

All the physical impressions that a person makes on us, and all the natural attractions, aversions and opinions that these arouse in us, have little to do with the phenomena of Spirit. For this same reason, they have little to do with the process of spiritual healing, so focusing on these distractions actually hinders the shaman's ability to become a hollow bone. Each shaman's experience of these phenomena differs, and different individuals tend to develop different sensory modalities that are innate to them. One shaman may more strongly visualize, while another may sense more viscerally, or may have strong auditory sensations or mental impressions. In any event, what matters here is that a shaman can "see" and communicate with wandering spirits and with Spirit Guides, Power Animals, and other beings in non-ordinary reality. Indeed, it is the very act of being able to "see" this invisible non-ordinary reality that makes the shaman's work seem so "magical."

Chapter III

Prelude to Depossession — Who Finds Help, and How

If we have a toothache, we go to a dentist. But when there's a psychological or emotional problem, we face a baffling array of possibilities. There are psychiatrists, of course, and these come in "schools" that have very different approaches and techniques. Then there are psychologists, who also represent a wide array of skill sets and philosophies. The aim of many psychological approaches is to help one cultivate better thoughts and habits, while giving little thought to the origin of the problem. Others suggest a prolonged therapist-client relationship, with the aim of insight and change over time. And of course, pharmaceutical drugs are often prescribed, to modify the client's chemistry in ways that are considered helpful.

To be sure, there are gifted therapists of many kinds who are helping people in wonderful ways. But if we consider the question of what is actually causing one's problem, these professionals typically offer theory, but not resolution. And when a person is host to an intrusive spirit, and begins to exhibit troubling or aberrant behavior, these approaches are palliative at best, and in no way address, let alone remove the cause of the problem. Shamanic depossession, though, with appropriate follow-up healing, *can* remove the problem.

Remove the problem? Yes, I know… This is a stunning idea, one that many people have trouble believing.

Modern psychology has led us to believe that psychological problems have a long background, and that even their partial resolution has a prolonged future. Indeed, it is commonly assumed that causes lie buried in the mists of time, in uncharted regions of a nebulously defined psyche. Shamanic healing, though, is based upon a radically different model. Not only does it offer an effective alternative approach to treatment, but in certain cases, it offers the best and possibly only promise of success. How, though, does one know if shamanic healing is called for?

Symptoms of Possession

It's not hard to draw up a long list of symptoms that have been experientially traced to possession, and cured by depossession. This list includes mental illnesses of many kinds, physical illnesses of many kinds, energy blocks, emotional distress, addictions, negativity, weakness, phobias, and identity and gender confusion. People are often curious to know how these different symptoms express the character of the intrusive spirit, and how this translates in the host's experience. As you can well imagine, this is an area that's ripe for fascinating stories and speculation of all kinds. When people ask me about how symptoms are related to the intrusive spirit, I usually disappoint them. For I tell them that I have little interest in "working backwards" from symptomology, because it contributes nothing to my ability to perform a successful depossession. Indeed, I find it only a distraction. Why do I say this?

If my spiritual diagnosis (which I will explain next) indicates a case of possession, my interest is in going directly to the source of that problem, confident that once I have enabled the lost soul to move on, this will relieve whatever symptoms have been associated with it. Typically, in conjunction with follow-up work that addresses the power loss that was there in the first place, this alleviates the complaint that the client has presented me, as well as other associated complaints they may not have presented. None of what I do, then, from start to finish, has the least basis in symptomology. By directly addressing the source of the problem, I am able to bypass all of that.

This approach also keeps things simpler and surer, since the subject of symptoms is a slippery terrain with many variables one can never be sure of anyway. For example, if a person keeps hearing voices telling them to do something outrageous or even violent, I need to look past such symptoms, because my concern is with dealing with the **cause** of those voices. Interestingly, symptoms do become a subject of interest after the intrusive spirit has been moved out. Having suffered these symptoms for some time, the client can empirically verify whether or not there has been a positive change. At that point, they become of interest to the client as a measure of their healing, as I explain in Chapter 6, but not as a meaningful aspect of their depossession.

Does this mean that I don't care about the client's symptoms? Heavens, no. I am continually, even daily, moved by the suffering, endurance, courage, and tenacity of my clients, who have deeply impressed me with the depths of the human spirit. When I meet a client, I listen to their story - in however much detail, and with as much emotional expression as they need in order to tell it. I want to know this fellow human being who has come to me! In this larger sense I may ask questions about their symptoms, but I do so not because this sheds any light on the healing I need to do. I do so because it creates a bond of understanding and trust between us. And that, of course, is no small thing. Though it may not relate directly to the "action" of my healing work, I can think of nothing more conducive to successful healing than a heartfelt human relationship between the client and healer. At the same time, it is important that the shaman's empathy does not interfere with his or her capacity to become a "hollow bone" through with the Compassionate Spirits perform their healing.

Spiritual Diagnosis

Depossession is only needed when a person has become host to an intrusive spirit. So - if a person is struggling with a psychological, emotional, or health problem, how can they know if this is due to possession, and not to some other psychological or physical cause? Some people, I have found, intuitively feel that they are in the grip of possession - and they may be right or they may be wrong. Others may never have even entertained the possibility. Clearly, then, there must be a process of diagnosis, in which it is determined whether there is, in fact, a possessing spirit that is contributing to the client's problems. And so, just as a medical doctor performs a diagnosis to determine what treatment is called for, so too does a shaman perform a diagnosis, albeit in a more mystical, but highly effective manner. In this, as in all things, the shaman does not work humanly, alone, but works with Spirit.

First, the shaman obtains the client's permission to proceed with the spiritual diagnosis. Once this is given, the shaman "journeys" to non-ordinary reality, the spiritual realm where he communicates with his or her Spirit Guides or Power Animals with whom he has developed strong relationships or alliances. Just as a doctor might have a variety of colleagues with whom he consults to resolve different kinds of problems, so too does the shaman request the help of specific allies who have agreed to help with specific types of situations. Thus, it is principally these Spirits who do the diagnostic work, with the shaman acting as a "hollow bone." A diagnostic journey is a specific journey that the shaman takes in order to meet such a Spirit Guide or Guides, whom he then asks questions regarding the nature of a specific problem, and what can be done to alleviate it.

The reply that is received will give the specific steps that must be taken, which may include multiple and different types of healing, as well as the order in which they should take place. Once this journey is complete, the shaman then has his road map, his prescription, so to speak. This spiritual diagnosis may also include other forms of healing, as well, such as soul retrieval and the extraction of intrusions. In some cases, a host may be harboring two or three possessing spirits. One may be lodged more deeply than the others, hiding behind them, so to speak, so it may take multiple sessions to clear the way before this spirit can be dealt with. Spiritual diagnosis and healing is not intended to resolve problems that can be addressed by allopathic medicine. I make sure that the client understands that I only address the spiritual causes of disharmony, and do not ever offer medical advice. If they are describing debilitating symptoms that may be causing a physical problem, I may ask my client when he or she last saw a doctor, since any number of other factors may be contributing to their distress. In such a case, my client may pursue a medical approach that is supplementary to their work with me, for there is no conflict between the two.

From his diagnostic journey, then, the shaman clearly knows whether or not possession is playing a role in the problem that the client presents. And if it does, he also knows whether depossession is necessary. You will ask, of course: If there **is** an invasive spirit, how can depossession **not** be necessary? To this I can only say that this is something I can neither understand nor decide upon. As I have tried to make clear, the shaman serves as a vehicle for healing; the healing that takes place is not an act of personal will as we commonly understand it. As a generalization, I can say that not all disease is necessarily bad, and that some learning process may be served by a person's continued possession. But this is not mine to decide in terms of a particular person. What I can also say, and this quite definitely, is that I have learned to trust in the beneficent intention of the Helping Spirits, and in the precise calibration of their response to our soul's true needs. In short, I listen to what Spirit tells me.

How do I know that what they tell me is authoritative? I know it is authoritative because it works. If it didn't produce real and positive results, I would do not do this work. Nor, I would add, would shamanic depossession be practiced in spiritual traditions world-wide throughout all of recorded history. As Stanislov Groff said with regard to metaphysical healing, "there can be understanding without results, and results without understanding." While this statement may raise the eyebrows of modern men and women, it will make perfect sense to whoever has been sufficiently humbled by the great Mystery in which we live.

In some cases in which depossession has been indicated by the Spirits, I discuss the concept with the client if I feel that they are emotionally prepared. If a person has come to me for the healing of physical or emotional problems, I may talk about "working with spirits," without actually mentioning the word depossession. Just as a psychologist shares perceptions with the client that are attuned to the client's emotional state and needs, so too does the shaman work intuitively within the crucible of trust that has been established. The first-hand account of a depossession that I performed, at the end of this book, illustrates this principle quite well.

Once I have established that depossession would be helpful, we might proceed with it directly, or depending upon the situation, make an appointment for another session. In any event, this spiritual diagnosis is an auspicious moment, for possession is the underlying cause of many problems that even the best-intentioned psychologist or doctor simply cannot resolve. At this point, the shamanic healer is truly "the right tool for the job," and can be a blessing to both the client as well as the lost soul.

✦

How People Find their Way to Shamanic Healing

So – if person is experiencing some form of suffering or distress, how do they find their way to shamanic healing? This happens differently for different people. Some are immediately attracted to the idea or to the trappings of shamanism, often based on their sympathies or contact with Native American traditions. Others have read something on the subject that was provocative, inspiring, or convincing. There are a number of good books out there, and there is lots of good material on the internet. Many shamans now have web-sites, and many non-practitioners are now writing on the subject, as well. That said, there is plenty of naïve nonsense, sheer fiction, and sensational stuff out there. This is why I've included a bibliography in Chapter 8. There, you will find some sources of clearly written, authoritative material on different aspects of shamanism. This should give you a sound basic overview of the subject, and get you started with the kind of authentic material you deserve.

People find their way to shamanism in other ways, as well. They may receive some kind of shock or inner experience that tells them that shamanism is how they will be healed. They may trust in a friend or relative who has experienced shamanic healing, or who has developed an interest in it. Others may be attracted to a lecture or workshop. Some people are brought to shamanism by desperation. They've tried the allopathic doctors. They've tried the diets and the herbal cures. They've tried every approach under the sun *but have not gotten results.*

In this regard, I really must say: It's unfortunate that a form of healing that is so personal, natural, effective, humane, non-invasive, and inexpensive has been, until the current resurgence starting in the late 60's, on the fringes of society, and is so often regarded with doubt in our culture. We can only be grateful that the tide is turning, as people are waking up to the deeper currents of the world's spiritual traditions. That said, given where we are today as a culture, people's initial approach to shamanic healing often entails a learning process, a process of discovery.

Getting Comfortable with Shamanism

B ecause shamanism is new to most people, they may need to develop trust in it. They must overcome different kinds of reservations they may have, which I quite understand. I was once having phone conversations with a man who expressed a strong interest in being healed, but was holding off due to his reticence about shamanism. Then one night he had a dream. In the dream it was late at night, and he was alone in a house in the woods, on a secluded property far from anyone else. Hearing the sound of a motor outside, he went to the window with trepidation. Who could it be at this hour? Pulling up to the house was a big old American jalopy, and by the glow of the headlights, he could see that the car was packed full, with six big, mature, easy-going American Indian men seated inside. His dream began on a forbidding note, but it ended with warm, even comical overtones. He awoke from the dream with a start.

He called me the next day and told me the dream.

"What do you make of it?" he asked.

"What do **you** make of it?" I asked in return. This was the turning point for him, as he saw this as a message from Spirit, and since he associated shamanism with Native American Indians, he decided to ask for an appointment. Interestingly during our work together he developed an emotional bond with the Spirits of American Indians, and we ended up helping rid this man of some strongly troubling issues, for which he is grateful to this day.

For another tentative client, the sticking point was the veracity of power animals. She just didn't see what animals could have to do with healing or spirituality. She too had a dream. In the dream she was shocked to find that a fox was creeping close to her, which she chased away, shouting loudly and filled with fear. The fox retreated just a short distance though, and then huddled close to the ground, looking up at her. She charged again, again stomping violently and shouting. Again the fox retreated, but again, only so far. And again it huddled down low and looked straight up at her.

This strange behavior put a brake on her momentum. She did not charge a third time. Instead, she looked the fox straight in the eyes. There, she was surprised to see eyes and a face filled with a gentleness, kindness, and sympathy that expressed qualities that struck deep into her heart. Seeing this, she wondered why she had charged the fox with such wrath and violence. She awoke in her bed and sat up, as her behavior in the dream filled her with sorrow. Overcome with emotion, she inwardly apologized to the fox, weeping hot tears at her estrangement from such goodness. She, too, was now ready for shamanic healing.

To anyone reading this book who has similar reservations, I would simply suggest that you make yourself available to the shamanic influences that have already found their way to you. This could involve reading a book on shamanism, looking at pictures, having vivid dreams of animals, or simply talking about the subject with friends or other people. It might simply involve musing on the reservations that worry you – what they represent, and where they come from.

Choosing a Shaman

When you are ready to move forward, your choice of a shaman is an important matter. The first reason your choice is important is that you want real results. A dabbler or self-styled pseudo-shaman will not produce these. The second reason, which is no less important, is that you are entrusting yourself to another person's care on the level of your soul. You want to choose quite carefully, then.

There are many currents of shamanic practice in the world today: many teachings, and many schools that have developed in different countries, ethnic groups, and religions. Though I am familiar with a number of these, my knowledge is not systematic, and I am in no position to act as an arbiter of these things. From my personal experience, though, I can say that a good place to begin is the Foundation for Shamanic Studies, which is where I received my own training. I can vouch for both the seriousness and integrity of the Foundation's training, and the quality and effectiveness of its graduates, many of whom I know, and have continued to work with. In Chapter 8 you can find contact information for the Foundation, and for Sandra Ingerman, both of whom offer a list of graduates who are currently practicing.

Whether you contact someone through the Foundation, or go to a healer from another tradition to whom you feel attracted, the best advice I can give is this: take all the time you need, ask as many questions as you need to ask, listen to your intuition, follow your heart, and go with what is comfortable to you. Do not be afraid to speak to or visit several practitioners until you find one who feels right to you. Your trust in the healer plays a big part in the success you will experience. It is also true, as we saw with my dreamer, that even when you find the right person, you may experience conflicted feelings. Apart from the continued "strangeness" you may feel about shamanism, the shaman is a human being who will evoke human responses in you, as would any other professional you might work with closely. Thus, while you have every right to expect wonderful things, it is unrealistic to expect some white knight who fulfills your every expectation.

The Material Question

This subject would be incomplete without touching upon the idea of payment. A good shaman is a skilled professional who offers a valuable service. In traditional cultures, the shaman was often well off, as people held the unique services they offered in high esteem because shamans produced results. Most shamans today charge fees that are in the range of other good healing professionals, both mainstream and alternative. I haven't studied the matter, but for sure there's a "high end" and a "low end" - and these do not necessarily correspond to the quality of care one receives. I know shamans who also work on a sliding scale, or even with barter, in the case of clients who have financial difficulties. In Spiritist churches, whose members practice spiritual healing that includes what they call "dis-possession," no fees are ever charged. The Spiritist tradition, which originates in Brazil but is now growing in the U.S., considers healing to be an expression of their religion, which cannot be an object of commerce. In any case, I have gratefully observed that the "commerce" of shamanism is not based upon unscrupulous profit. It is typically imbued with a respectful awareness that reflects the integrity and sincere disposition of all concerned.

I must also add that there are unscrupulous pseudo-shamans and self-styled mystic healers of different stripes who may or may not know what they are doing, and may charge exorbitant or even outrageous fees. Whether self-deluded or predatory, they are poised to exploit people who are desperate or naive. Knowing this, if you use the nose of a serpent and the heart of a dove, you should be able to easily recognize and avoid such people.

Now that we understand the context in which depossession takes place in our culture, and the different ways people find their way to shamanic healing, we are ready to look at the act of depossession itself, which is the subject of the next chapter.

Chapter IV

The Act of Depossession

The Setting — Ritual and Ceremony

Depossession is a sacred act that has great meaning for the client, and no less for the lost soul. As such, it merits a setting that dignifies the process and is conducive to its success. There are certain ways in common that today's shamans go about doing this. The first is to provide for the client's ease and comfort. It is not uncommon to find a clean, quiet, private space, soft lighting, and comfortable furnishings, which could be in a home or office. This could also, and often does include much more, such as cushions, carpets, and the display of sacred art and artifacts, creating an environment that is not just safe and comfortable, but beautiful and meaningful as well. The shaman will often burn some sacred herbs during various healing ceremonies, at times using invocations and songs, and rattles and drums to call in compassionate spirits in order to orchestrate the healing.

More important than the setting, though, is the psychological and emotional space that the shaman provides. This takes place at the gut level of trust, and though many words may be exchanged, the feeling of safety, of not being judged, of being in good hands, is largely felt at a non-verbal level. As I said earlier, I am happy to share as many words as are needed for my client and me to forge a warm human bond. The nonverbal exchange underlying these words, though, is the main event taking place.

There **is** one other important use of words, though, namely prayer and invocation. It is only fitting to state one's intentions, express one's sincerity and gratitude, and acknowledge the presence of the helping Spirits. Many cultures have understood that depossession is essentially a sacred rite, and it is best approached in that way. This prayerful invocation is quite different from prayer as it is often practiced, in that it is not an asking or a beseeching for the things we need. Rather, it is an expression of thankfulness for what we already have, and an acknowledgment of our humble stature before the Spirits, without whom we are truly powerless and small. Invocations and prayer take different forms for different shamans, and these are determined by the nature of the relationship and the agreements that the shaman has with particular Spirits.

The Act Itself

While every depossession has certain elements in common, no two cases are the same. They cannot be the same because depossession is a very personal event in which three dynamics interact:
- The knowledge, personality and capability of the healer, and the power of the healer's Helping Spirits,
- The character and disposition of the host,
- The character and disposition of the lost soul.

The healer orchestrates these dynamics in a changeable event that takes place in real time. As you can see, then, it's a process that requires real skill and sensitivity. Though the word "depossession" has a clinical sound, I can assure you that it is a profoundly human process.

I will now explain how the process takes place. I have been selective about what I share, because my intention is neither to whet nor satisfy my reader's every curiosity. Nor is this in any way a manual for amateur depossession. My goal is to help modern men and women appreciate the veracity of depossession, and its benign and beneficent nature, and to enable some readers to find the kind of help they are praying for, for themselves or their loved ones.

The spiritual diagnosis I described in Chapter 3 may have taken place in a session before the depossession, or it may immediately precede the depossession itself. As you will recall, on his diagnostic journey, the shaman is given a "road map" that might call for a specific sequence of healing sessions, and might also include extraction and/or soul retrieval, with depossession perhaps deferred to a later session. In this regard, the permission the client has given me to perform healing gives me some helpful flexibility within ethical boundaries.

After my diagnostic journey I don't generally tell the client that the spirit of a dead person has entered his or her energy field and needs to be moved on. Even for a sophisticated, spiritually prepared client, this idea can be highly charged and unhelpful. I may thus use other, less emotionally-charged words that suggest this idea. Because I've been given permission to heal, I am free to perform the various activities needed to bring about healing, while always continuing to clarify the parameters of that permission with the client. Let me say again, though: my bonding with the client at a gut and heart level is what sets the stage for all that follows, and it usually precludes the need for clinical explanation. Let us assume now, that I have a spiritual diagnosis of possession, that permission for healing was granted, and that the client has received any preliminary spiritual treatment that was called for. I am ready, then, to proceed.

A Basic Outline of the Process

Though depossession is a mystical event that has infinite nuances, it typically follows a basic structure of four phases.

1) **Engaging the Spirit Helpers** - The shaman moves through a "portal" or entrance into non-ordinary reality, where he makes contact with his Spirit Helpers, who are then poised to assist him.

2) **Engaging the Lost Soul** – The shaman orchestrates the intrusive spirit's agreement to vacate the host and move on from the earth plane (the Middle World). This vacating, this moving out, is always done with the possessing spirit's full agreement.

3) **Helping the Lost Soul Cross Over** – With his Spirit Helpers, the shaman assists the lost soul in actually crossing over.

4) **Return to the Client** – The shaman tends to the needs of the client, then brings the session to a close.

Let's look at these four phases in more detail now.

Engaging the Spirit Helpers

For an experienced shaman, crossing the portal into non-ordinary reality and meeting his Spirit Helpers is not like flying blind through clouds and mist in an adventure movie. While it **does** feel adventurous, it is a voluntary journey to a definite place he has been before, to meet spirits with whom he has a well-established working relationship. I wish I could convey to you how comforting and beautiful it is each time that I make this contact. Every time I see the Compassionate Helping Spirits, my heart melts from the grandeur and the depth of empathy that I feel in them.

An experienced shaman has a number of Spirit Helpers whom he calls on for different purposes. Depossession is one such purpose, and during a depossession, there may be several Spirits in attendance, which may also include the spirits of Archangels. Once these Spirits are poised to work with me, the stage is set for the next phase, in which I engage in a respectful exchange with the lost soul, during which I explain why it is in his or her best interest to move on, and ultimately achieve this goal with their agreement.

Although some traditions employ force, threats, or even trickery to achieve this, my own tradition places a great emphasis on the importance of respect and non-judgment for these often-lost souls. Happily, we are able to obtain excellent results by employing gentle but powerful heart-centered persuasion.

Establishing Communication with the Invasive Spirit

At this point, although my client is there with me, expecting something, my task at hand now lies primarily with the invasive spirit. Depending upon my client, there are two possible approaches I can take to establish communication with the invasive spirit. This communication takes place at the same verbal level we commonly engage in conversation, while it is simultaneously accompanied by shamanic vision and perception of the intrusive spirit.

In the case that I notice traits in my client that indicate that they might have the ability to channel, I ask if they would mind "stepping aside" so that the possessing spirit can come through. My conversation with the possessing spirit, which I will soon describe, would then take place with the client serving as a kind of middleman through which the possessing spirit speaks. You may naturally wonder how a person with no experience of this kind is able to do this. Some non-shamanic healers who practice different forms of depossession that are called "spirit clearing," "entity removal," etc. may use hypnotism or relaxation techniques to make this possible.

I have found that my clients' good intentions and general willingness usually enables them to "step aside" and let the possessing spirit speak using their voice. While this is something they might not normally do, they can usually do so in a positively structured ritual setting in which there are lots of spirit helpers to ensure success. When we speak about this at the end of the session, the client will often express surprise, saying something like, "I can't believe I just did that!" or "I can't believe those words just came out of my mouth!" or "Wow, what was that voice all about? It surely wasn't mine!"

In the case that my client is not able to step aside, I will usually call in a colleague who is able to communicate and act as a channel for spirits. Thus, whether the client is acting as a "middleman" or a third person is present to serve that function, I am now ready to begin.

Let us say, for example, that a client had come to me with the complaint of chronic and overwhelming bursts of anger, and that part of the shamanic healing calls for a depossession. I might continue, then, along the following lines:

"If anger had a shape, what shape would it be?"
"A big irregular cloud," they say.
"And if it had a color, what color would it be?"
"Dark, like charcoal."
"If this anger had a person's name, what name would you give it?"
"Frank."

"Ok… so this anger has the shape of a big irregular cloud, its color is dark charcoal, and its name is Frank. So… now I would like you to step aside, please, and I would like to talk to Frank. Please let Frank come through now, and use your voice."

At this point, there is an experienced shaman on hand, and abundant spiritual help and power is present with my helping spirits. It is this atmosphere of safety and strength that facilitates and makes possible what follows.

"Can I please speak to Frank now?"

The word "yes" is then uttered from the client's mouth

"My name is Peter. It's good to meet you, Frank."

At this point, it becomes clear to me that "Frank," the possessing spirit, is now actively present and is actually speaking through the client or invited medium. From this point forward, the tone of the client's or medium's voice usually changes, and I am able to see clearly and sense the presence of the possessing spirit. There is no doubt about it. It is a fact that I have now confirmed.

The stage is now set for me to continue to communicate with that spirit.

Engaging the Possessing Spirit

I now set out to engage that spirit in a human conversation. At first, the spirit is usually reluctant to do so; they are fearful and confused, which fills me with compassion, for they may feel distrust regarding the shaman's appearance and intervention. In more challenging and rare cases, the spirit may even challenge me with a barrage of vulgar contempt, something on the order of "Who the ★★★★ **are** you and what the ★★★★ do you want?" On the other hand, there are also possessing spirits who just start chatting away, without guardedness or reserve, as if we'd just met at a party. Regardless of how I am received, I forge ahead with the conversation, equipped with strategies for dealing with the full range of possibilities. I would reiterate here that even as there may be phases to the process, it is a dynamic real-time event in which I essentially deal with what is before me.

Remember now, that this spirit may not know that they have died. It is living a kind of twilit life huddled within another person, where it has no past and no future, and no context for reflection. I therefore approach this spirit just as I would a stranger on a street corner: with calmness, simplicity, and respect. I first greet the Spirit and tell them that my name is Peter. I then proceed to ask some very simple questions. These are "icebreakers" which, as we will soon see, experience has shown are able to move the dialogue in a fruitful direction. While there is certainly no "script" involved in our dialogue, here too, there are several typical phases in the conversation that tend to comprise a design.

I will next offer you an example of such a dialogue. *Please note that it is not a verbatim transcript of an actual depossession.* Rather, it is a distilled composite that illustrates the main phases and themes of my dialogue with the possessing spirit. This composite, which is drawn from my experience, illustrates the key principles that are involved.

🦅 🦅 🦅

I was giving a two-day workshop on shamanism in a region of Europe that had been the site of trench warfare in World War I. A young woman who came to the workshop was quite agitated and jumpy, and kept asking questions in an aggressive and almost raging manner. On the first day she took up much too much space with her interruptions and attitude; I considered asking her privately to leave the course. Not feeling quite right about that, I resolved to be compassionate and accommodate her as best I could, while not compromising the experience of the rest of the participants. That evening, she asked if she could speak to me in private.

Out on the balcony, she told me that she was jumping out of her skin with nervousness and had developed a smoking habit that was "burning her up." "How much do you smoke?" I asked. "Four packs a day," she said. And she then gave way to sharing with me some of the suffering that clearly lay beneath her irritating behavior. The rather desperate and sincere way she confided in me and asked for help, confirmed my intuition about not asking her to leave the course. She asked me if there was anything I could do to help heal her, which led to our scheduling a private session together.

In that session, I first journeyed to non-ordinary reality, where I contacted my Helping Spirits. This was my diagnostic journey, in which it was shown to me that there was, in fact, an obsessing spirit. I also asked if they could help my client step aside. I was assured that they would do so. As I described above, I asked the woman if she would not mind "stepping aside," which she did. At this point, then, with the steps of permission and spiritual diagnosis taken care of, and with the Compassionate Spirits in attendance, I turned my attention to the obsessing spirit inside her.

First, I introduced myself.

"Hello. My name is Peter." I said. *"Would you mind telling me your name?"*
"Sandro."
"Good to meet you, Sandro. How old you are, Sandro?"
"I'm twenty-seven."
"Sandro, can you tell me the last thing you remember doing?"
"Me? I was a soldier."
"Where were you a soldier?"
"Lots of places."
"Can you name one place for me?"
"It was at Gallipoli."
"What were you doing there?"
"I was just standing there in a trench, smoking a cigarette during a break, between mortar bombings."
"And after that...?"
"I don't know."
"So you're not there, at Gallipoli, anymore...?"
"I guess not..."

This polite but persistent questioning about the circumstances of the spirit's death is important, as it represents the first breach in the spirit's ignorance of its present situation. I do not tell the possessing spirit that it is dead, though. This could easily evoke a reaction or denial that would create agitation, which would not at all be helpful. I have, however, begun to lay the groundwork for the spirit to arrive at an implicit understanding that they are no longer in their body as before.

> *"So tell me," I say… "How do you like it where you are now?"*
> *"It's o.k."*
> *"What do you like about it?"*
> *"I'm here with this nice lady and we go out for a smoke all the time."*

Once our dialogue is established, I find a way to help the spirit understand that they are not where they should be. Again, this cannot be done directly, for they do not understand their true circumstance. Indeed, this soldier's naiveté seemed remarkable, as this "nice lady" who was such a pleasant smoking companion seemed to satisfy the needs of his existence.

The next phase of our dialogue continues what is called 'softening of the spirit.' Contrary to our foolish misconceptions, many of these lost souls harbor the same decent impulses toward goodness, wholeness, and integration as you and I. This seems to be a basic "instinct" of the human soul that is never quite extinguished, though it can certainly remain buried in the current circumstance of a soul who is lost. And yet – despite their confusion, despite their inability to understand their situation, such lost souls typically have a latent impulse to move on.

This basic "instinct," though, may also be so deeply buried that I encounter not a glimmer of goodness or trust. There are also invasive spirits who know quite well that they are dead, and want very much to continue their uninvited stay in the Middle World of non–ordinary reality, where they can continue to wreak all kinds of havoc, as is their bent. Between these two poles of lost but decent possessing spirits, and intentionally malicious ones, there is every degree in between. My job is to understand the type of spirit I am dealing with, to not be fazed if it appears hostile, and to continue forward, undaunted.

"Are you comfortable here?"
"Kind of. I suppose. I mean… I guess so."
"Are you happy? I mean… are you really happy where you are now?"
"I guess… well… not exactly. Not really, not most of the time."

This exchange illustrates another key way in which our carica-tured images mislead us. We've been led to imagine that these lost souls are having some kind of gleeful experience as the masterful pup-peteer of their human host. When you actually "meet" many of these spirits though, believe me: this image just falls to pieces. There is and can be no enduring satisfaction in their situation, and on some level, quite fortunately, the lost soul often knows this. At the other end of the spectrum, though, as I indicated above, there is also the opposite pole, in which an invasive spirit exerts the power it has over its host with deliberate intention, and quite enjoys its mastery of the small world of that one person.

Regardless of what I encounter, I now steer the conversation in a new direction.

"Sandro… I really feel your unhappiness and would like to help you. What if I could take you to a place where you can be happy? I mean really happy. All the time… Would you want to go there?"
"But I don't know of such a place," would be a typical response of a possessing spirit who is not overtly hostile.
Or: *"What the **** are you talking about…?"* might be the challenge of one who is, let's say, rather less receptive.

Again… whatever the case, I forge on.
"I **do** know of such a place, and I can take you there. It's a place where there is only beauty, only love, and people who want the best for you, all the time… I can take you there. I've taken lots of other people there before and they are very happy now."

There are variations on how I might present this positive, invit-ing, and best of all, true world that actually exists. In some cases, this is such an attractive prospect that the rest of the depossession proceeds with relative ease. But let's consider now the scenario in which the possessing soul is reluctant, resistant, and still does not want to leave. Let's say that my soldier is not biting. He's not interested in what I have to offer. If I arrive at an impasse, I check with my Spirit guide, just as one might consult a specialist in a team of doctors. I may then receive an idea, or a question to ask, which may be something I would not have thought of asking on my own, but which provides exactly the wedge or leverage I need in order to take the next step. The beauty and adventure of this is that I never know what will happen next; there is no script. And it is for this reason that the shaman needs to have guidance from Spirit.

At this point I continue with my practice of softening the spirit – and this is important - always without the least harshness or aggression. I present myself with straightforward directness, but my plan is to succeed based on harmony and agreement between us, and that is not achieved by means of force, threats, or condemnation. I begin, then, to play what is often one of my trump cards. I begin by helping the spirit make an emotional connection to a real person they were fond of in life.

"Sandro… can you tell me about your parents? Are they still alive?"

In the case of Sandro, who died in World War I, there would be no reason to ask such a question since his parents have obviously passed over. I include it here, though, on account of the principle it illustrates in the common cases in which the spirit's death has been more recent. In that case, if the answer is 'yes,' I ask: *"How about your grandparents? Did you have a favorite grandmother or grandfather? Did they pass away while you were young…?"*

With these questions I lead the spirit to specify someone in their life who was dear to them, who they loved, and who they also know has passed on. In all of this, with sincere kindness and empathy, I try to revive and evoke real feelings of affection that they once experienced but have become frozen in a heart that has become confused.

I now return to my earlier tack, but with a trump card I didn't play before.

In this example, my soldier is talking to me, and he's listening – I can see that. But he's still not convinced. I can see and feel his resistance. I have set the stage though, for the emotional contact with his ancestors that will typically motivate a lost soul to move on to the other side, if not at once, then later.

Let's say, though, that I am dealing with a really stubborn and entrenched spirit. Perhaps it is my smoking soldier who is just plain resistant. Or perhaps it is a downright malicious spirit who has shown very little sign of softening. At this point I may take a more forward step – once again: always with good heart. I might ask him to describe himself... what he looks like, his hair color, the color of his eyes, etc. I might also ask him to describe his garb. And if he still shows no intention to leave his host, I will say something like:

> "So you told me you have green eyes and a beard, and that your hair color is brown, yes?... o.k., then... let me ask you a question: 'Who is that, then?' I ask the possessing soul, holding up a mirror in front of my client's eyes. 'Look at it closely...is that you?'"
>
> "Well no, that's not me... I don't know... It's not me, though."
>
> "Do you know why you are not seeing your own face in that mirror? Let me tell you why. The image you are seeing is that of the young lady you smoke with. She has come to see me because she needs my help, because she's not at all happy now. In fact, she is really suffering, and all this smoking you are forcing her to do is actually killing her, and she's not enjoying it one bit...
>
> "Listen Sandro... something happened to you at Gallipoli. But you and I are talking, so you still exist, but as you can see, you are with this lady now, in her body. So you are actually hurting her... now is that what you want to do?"

The response from a callous spirit could take many forms, but in this case, Sandro's response was encouraging:

> "Well no... not really. I don't want to hurt her. I just want a buddy to smoke with," he replied.
>
> "I understand that. But you are causing this lady harm even though you don't mean to, and you are using her body to do so. Listen: you've told me that you are really not happy here anyway, so let's make a deal: you leave this nice lady in peace so she won't be so nervous and

upset and you stop hurting her… If you agree to do that, I promise to take you to that place I told you about. The place where there is only love, and where your relatives live, waiting for you…."

As gently but firmly as possible, I nudge the lost soul toward an understanding, on the simplest human level, that they are not where they belong, and that they are causing another person to suffer, as well. Having answered my previous questions that described the situation previous to the point of death, the spirit is starting to get the picture. It is now time to lay down my best trump card.

I call upon the Helping Spirits to locate the person for whom the possessing spirit expressed fondness and affection. In this soldier's case, it was a favorite aunt. I open a portal and call upon my Spirit Guides, who are specialized in these matters, and are able to offer incentive that is far more convincing than all that I have offered thus far. In response, my Helping Spirits locate the soldier's aunt. This does not take long at all, for in non-ordinary reality, things happen "at the speed of intention."

"I'm going to open up a circle of light for you," I tell the soldier. "Up here… take a look. Can you see that light? There's someone I'd like you to meet. Look, up here… can you see her up there, right at the edge of the circle?"

The soldier looks up, and there he sees his favorite aunt, who is waiting, welcomingly, at the edge of the portal to the Other Side. Not only does he see this dear human figure, but he also sees an Archangel and whichever other Spirits are in attendance. His recognition of his aunt, the inviting portal of light, and the sight of actual Angels, resplendent, real, and shining with the deepest empathy and purest love imaginable, is an irresistible combination.

"C'mon," I say, "give me your hand. Let me take you there."

I extend my hand and guide the soldier to the portal. Although this takes place in non-ordinary reality, I feel his hand quite definitely, just as I would your hand or anybody's hand. I then entrust him to the beautiful custody of the Spirits, who lead him through the portal, to the Other Side. I then close the portal with great intention, to bring closure to the event. Once the portal is closed, the depossession is over. It has been a success. At this point, my work and my relationship with this wandering soul is over. It does not continue in any way, shape or fashion.

How long did the depossession take? Depending on the resistance I encountered, anywhere from ten minutes to an hour or, at times, longer. During the entire process I worked hard to act appropriately in both worlds from which I was receiving information: that of non-ordinary reality, and that of my client. In the end, when I look back on all of it and try to review how it all took place, I am myself often amazed by many aspects of it. How did I know to say that? What inspired me to make that gesture at that moment? No matter how much I have learned and how often I have performed depossession, there is always an element of wonder to this mystical process that has such practical results.

Return to the Client

During this time, the client may have experienced any number of feelings or sensations. Although I am in a voluntarily altered state of consciousness, I remain very aware of everything that is happening around me. Indeed, one of the shaman's key talents consists in being able to intelligently and effectively function in two worlds at once. Thus, I have been aware of my client throughout this exchange, and when called for, may have reassured them with words, when needed, or by taking their hand, etc. I also try to mollify any negative emotions the client may experience or express by assuring them that that they are safe. The possessing spirit is privy to the thoughts and feelings of the client, so if the client experiences or expresses negativity of any kind, this undermines the atmosphere of harmony and trust that I am trying to cultivate. It's also true that some possessing spirits thrive on negative emotions, and I do not want to feed this tendency, since this will only exacerbate their resistance, and the client will then suffer their agitation. This is why the harmonious setting, the ceremonial aspect of the process, my Helping Spirits, and my orchestration of the depossession all work together to create a successful outcome.

Once the possessing spirit is gone, an immediate effect can be seen in the client. The most general result is that I see a new vitality in the person. They seem more fully present, as a certain absentness is replaced by a more active presence. The light is on again. For some, this transition may cause emotions of many kinds to well up. People sometimes cry in the wake of their depossession, but when they do, these are usually tears of joy, gratitude, and relief, as they feel a new sense of lightness as a burden has been lifted.

There can be a wide range of expression, though, which can sometimes be surprising. As he shares in his first-hand account in Chapter 7, one client of mine found himself passionately pounding the floor with his fists, crying out "I've never lived!" over and over again. It turns out that I had helped a spirit cross over who had invaded and inhabited his body since early childhood. In order not to scare the client, I had only told him we would be "continuing with the healing." I had not even mentioned the word 'depossession.' Yet in the catharsis that he experienced, on an emotional level he knew quite well what had happened.

In any case, a person who has been depossessed has just had a very significant inner experience. Since the time they walked in the door, they have been purged of an influence that has been impacting their mind, body, and feelings day in, day out, and often for a very long time. For virtually everyone, there is an emotional sense that something "big" has happened. As I mentioned earlier, I do not share any of the more specific or unsavory details of the experience with my client. I do, however, distill the energetic event that has just occurred into a healing story. I weave a story full of positive hope for the future; hope is often something they have lacked for some time. The client then has an inspirational story that begins to modify how they see themselves, which then starts to constructively shape their future and their interaction with others. This story is not my own invention. Rather, it is woven from the client's own experience, to help them elaborate a new vision in full possession of their newfound energy and the freedom to live life to its fullest potential. It is important to mention here, that the nature of the stories that we create for ourselves will determine where our life will take us as we create our new future.

Due to the work that takes place in my studio, it is filled with a heightened energy and a calming atmosphere in which the presence of Spirit can be felt. In every case, I keep the client with me and I talk with them, or just sit with them, until I feel the process has settled and they are able to leave. People may experience a dramatic contrast between how they feel before and after the session, and they may still be processing strong energies and raw feelings. For this reason I will often ask my client to bring a friend or family member with them. I want to be sure that they can adjust to the changes they have experienced, and that they have the support they need when they emerge from my studio into the less rarified energies of ordinary life.

One way that helps to bring closure and harmony to the experience is to end the session just as we began it, with ceremony and prayer. And this we do, often with fresh and heartfelt feeling, as we express our gratitude for the intervention of the Compassionate Spirits, without whom this blessed healing would not have taken place.

Epilogue: The Strength of the Shaman's Compassion

Not all shamans perform depossession. Just as doctors have specialties for which other doctors have no affinity, it's a distinct and unusual process that is not for everybody. As I shared in my introduction, I've had a natural and sincere curiosity about death since I was a child. I also have a degree in psychology, and a great love for people. Together, these give me a kind of strength as I enact the diplomacy involved in depossession, for I am acting straight from the heart, without force, without guile, and without manipulation. It is not unusual for me to tear up in my encounter with a lost soul, as I feel and contemplate the pain of their situation. I think that I am effective because my motives are clean and transparent.

I also do not feel that I am in any danger. This is not because an intrusive spirit does not pose a real danger. Quite the contrary: they have already proved dangerous to my client, and could also prove dangerous to someone who meddles in their circumstance without adequate preparation and protection. However, with my training, experience, and the presence of Spirits filling me with their power, I have no reason to feel unsafe. In addition, because I am seeing with my heart, I know that I am dealing with ignorance, not evil. To be sure, the situation can be pretty unsavory at times, and that's a very real side of things that I would not want to minimize. I don't see the point of sharing the details of it in a book, though, since this would only reinforce the fears and negative attitudes that I am trying to dispel here, and it does not characterize the majority of cases.

In any case, I don't allow whatever obstacles I encounter to override the fact that this is a suffering human spirit. This is the same decent, humane attitude you will find in any good nurse or doctor who faces challenging situations helping difficult people, yet remains committed to helping their fellow human beings. A shaman typically experiences deep sufferings, often from a very early age. And while the shaman may bear scars as a result of life's challenges, his heart, or her heart, has no calluses. How could it be otherwise, in a vocation to which one has been called by Spirit? Indeed, these sufferings create a compassion that is intimately linked to the ability to "see"; being a shaman and deep compassion go hand in hand.

🦅 🦅 🦅

I would next like to address the issues related the aftermath of a depossession, in which the client psychologically integrates the results of the process. But before doing so, in the next chapter I'd like to briefly explain how depossession differs from exorcism.

As a general principle, it is best to work positively in one's own affairs, and not busy oneself criticizing what others may be doing differently. However, since the aim of this book is to demystify depossession, I must necessarily contrast it with exorcism, with which it is quite commonly and quite wrongly confused. This is also a subject that most people find quite intriguing.

Chapter V

How Is Depossession Different from Exorcism?

The Catholic Church has always recognized the reality of possession, and exorcism, of course, is the practice it developed to address this reality. To this day, the Church trains selected priests in how to perform the rite, which has its own prerequisites, rituals, and liturgy. Our modern associations to exorcism quite misrepresent it, as they typically portray horrific possessions by demonic figures who utterly overwhelm their hosts with deranged behavior. The movie The Exorcist pretty much cast the mold in this regard. Leaving aside such sensational and caricatured cases, which primarily serve to sell books and movies, Catholic exorcism involves dynamics that are quite different from those of depossession as it is practiced in my tradition. Indeed, these dynamics are so different that the two practices can in no way be considered synonymous.

Two Approaches that are Very Different, Indeed

As you have read in these pages, in the shamanic view, the possessing soul is a confused human spirit who has become lost, and needs to be compassionately helped to move on from this level. There is no judgment of these souls (whose plight is, in fact, rather tragic), and their crossing to the Other Side is considered as much a positive outcome as is their departure from the host. In performing depossession, the shaman expresses his compassion for both parties, and is assisted by Divine Helpers. The Catholic model of exorcism is entirely different on all these counts.

First of all, in the Catholic conception, the possessing soul is always viewed as a demonic entity that Jesus Christ must cast back into Hell. This premise, of course, is contrary to our understanding in today's emerging spirituality. Not only does our more progressive understanding of "hell" preclude the existence of some realm of eternal damnation, it also precludes a punitive Jesus Christ who would authorize such condemnation. It goes without saying, then, that exorcism does not even consider, let alone accomplish, the successful crossing over of this "evil entity." In addition, the priest assumes a stern adversarial stance toward the possessing spirit, quite unlike the sincere communication established by a shamanic practitioner. Thus, the entire Catholic conception of depossession is so divorced from the actual human reality experienced by shamanic practitioners worldwide, that one doesn't know "whether to laugh or cry," as the saying goes.

Analogous to the shaman's diagnostic journey, the priest first performs an extensive inquiry to determine whether the person appealing for help is, in fact, the host of a possessing spirit. Since 1999, this inquiry process has also included a psychiatric examination, to rule out other psychological causes. Once a determination is made that there is a possessing spirit, exorcism moves forward in a process driven by fear and enacted by force, both subtle and overt, in which no love or respect is shown for the possessing spirit, who is viewed as "the devil." Along with its ritual aspects and prayers, the priest admonishes and threatens the lost soul as an adversary who must be overwhelmed with fear and vanquished. It is no wonder that exorcism is often a rocky process which, truth be told, often leaves the priest in bad shape in the end. And because the process is definitely upsetting to the possessing spirit, it is also upsetting to the person being depossessed. Imagine how **you** would feel and react if you didn't know that you were dead, didn't know where you were, and someone you didn't know accosted you, threw holy water at you, and threatened you with imprecations you didn't even understand and told that you will be cast back into hell for eternity!

From the client's viewpoint, perhaps it may ultimately not matter by what means they are liberated from the burden of the possessing spirit. That said, they are quite naturally inspired with trepidation by the prolonged formal diagnosis they must undergo, the rebuking stance assumed by the priest, and the negative feelings they experience simply by being formally in the pipeline for such a "spooky event" as exorcism. From the viewpoint of the lost soul spirit and the healer, though, there is a far greater difference between exorcism and depossession – and it is a difference that strikes deep into our moral sense of things.

✦

A Simple Analogy

This difference can be illustrated by a simple analogy. Imagine that I receive a call from a neighbor. She tells me she has been hearing disturbing sounds in her attic for some time. She's been scared to investigate, and it has gotten on her nerves so much that she's a nervous wreck and her health is run-down. She's heard I'm good at dealing with different kinds of people in tough and strange situations. "Do you think you can help?" she asks. "Let's give it a try," I say. And off I go to pay her a visit.

Mounting the stairs to her attic, I find that there is, in fact, someone living up there: a homeless squatter, it seems, who is lost, confused, and basically in sad shape – or hostile, belligerent, but still in basically sad shape. I take out my cell phone and make a few calls to some people I know who specialize in helping the homeless. I've worked with these specialists before, and no sooner do I call them than they are on their way to help out.

Turning back to the squatter, I respectfully strike up a simple conversation to earn their trust. I try to help them realize that there is a far superior living situation that's ready and waiting for them, and that I've even got friends downstairs who are waiting to bring them there. The conversation tacks this way and that, but the squatter is still resistant, maybe even hostile.

I make another phone call, and ask the squatter to take a look out the little window of the attic. There, on the sidewalk below, stands his favorite aunt, in the sunshine, waving to him. "Would you like to go to that wonderful situation I described to you earlier?" I ask. "It's where your aunt lives; we can go join her right now if you want." This works. The squatter takes my hand and accompanies me down the stairs. There, in the living room, waits a doctor, a social worker, and the squatter's favorite aunt. Gathered around the squatter, brimming with goodwill, these three well-intentioned people bring him to his proper home, which has been waiting for him since he first became lost, long ago.

My friend is grateful and relieved, the squatter is in good hands, and I've played my role of facilitator with a warm heart. Mission accomplished.

🦅 🦅 🦅

Let's apply this same scenario now, to a case of exorcism. In this scenario, my scared and distressed neighbor calls a priest, not a shamanic practitioner. The priest tells her that he must conduct a series of interviews with her. She must also undergo a psychiatric evaluation, to rule out other possible causes of her distress. Once he determines that the scary-sounding rite of "exorcism" is called for, a number of forms must be filled out to authorize this. At the end of this protracted preliminary process, the prospect of a mysterious exchange taking place in her attic has filled my neighbor with dread. She sticks with it though, for what alternative does she have?

When the priest finally comes to her house, he's bristling with hostile and negative expectations regarding this definitely demonic person who might be in the attic. He steels himself for the exchange and mounts the attic stairs, my neighbor close behind. Then, with a mixture of oaths, prayers, force and threats that my friend finds highly disturbing, and that sends the squatter into a commotion, the priest drives the terrified person (who never spoke a word nor was asked a word) down the stairs and out the front door. The squatter is last seen running at top speed, panicked, down the street.

Where is the squatter going? Well… who knows? And after all… who cares? He was definitely no good, right? And he's gone now. Mission accomplished!

"Mission accomplished?" Let's consider this question.

True - my friend no longer has a squatter in her attic. And even though she had to go through a protracted and unpleasant process, the vacating of the squatter is a real blessing. But what about the other two sides of the equation? Has the squatter been entrusted to compassionate people who will bring him to a better place, where he actually belongs, where he can be helped? No - he was driven out into the streets, into exactly the same situation he was in before settling into my friend's attic. What will he do there? Well again… who knows? And who really cares? Maybe he will find his way into someone else's attic, but that will be *their* problem – out of sight and mind of my neighbor and her priest.

As regards the priest, you can bet that he has performed the rite in good conscience – he has, after all, the sanction and tradition of the entire Catholic Church on his side. I have a problem, though, with the underlying assumptions and methods used in Exorcism. Here is the actual Latin verbiage used in the rite of exorcism, followed by its English translation:

Exorcizamos te,omnis immunde spiritus, omnis satainic potestas, omnis infernalis adversarii, omnis legio, omnis congretatio et secta diabolica, in nomine et virtute Domini nostril Jesu Christi, eradicare et effugare a Dei Ecclesia, ab animabus ad imaginem Dei conditis ac pretioso divini Agni sanguine redeptis. Non ultra audeas, serpens callidissime, decipere humanum genus, Dei Ecclesiam persegui, ac De electos excutere et crirare sicut triticum. Imperat tibi Deus altissimus, cui in magna tua superbia te simile haberi adhus praesumis; qui omnes hominess vult salvos fiery, et ad agnitionem veritatis venire.

We cast you out, every unclean spirit, every satanic power, every onslaught of the infernal adversary, every legion, every diabolical group and sect, in the name and by the power of our Lord Jesus Christ. We command you, be gone and fly far from the Church of God, from the souls made by God in His Image and redeemed by the Precious Blood of the Divine Lamb. No longer dare, cunning serpent, to deceive the human race, to persecute God's Church, to strike God's elect and to sift them as wheat. For the Most High God commands you,

He to Whom you once proudly presumed yourself equal; He Who wills all men to be saved and come to the knowledge of Truth commands you.

And believe me, it gets even more aggressive – to put it mildly – as the rite continues. The "devil spirit" is commanded to return to hell's eternal damnation.

In exorcism, the priest assumes such a harsh, adversarial stance – both within himself, and toward the wandering soul – that I could never, in good conscience, force myself to generate, let alone direct such aggression toward another. This is doubly the case since I know that a far better, more humane and thorough result can be achieved by calling on the best and most compassionate aspects of my nature. I am left with the conclusion, then, that exorcism is far less humane than depossession, which is rooted in forgiveness and concern for the lost soul. I would only add that I don't intend this as a negative judgment or a rebuke of the entire Catholic Church, which serves many worthwhile causes for good on this earth... and shamans try not to judge in such matters.

🦅 🦅 🦅

I would think this a bitter subject if I did not understand that we are in a wonderful time of great change, in which centuries-old attitudes and feelings are melting away as a new model of humanity emerges. We can see this in many arenas of life in which new and humane perspectives are replacing rigid old forms. Another particularly relevant example of this comes to mind...

For thousands of years it was believed that the only way to domesticate a wild horse is to lasso it, bind it so tightly in ropes that it is lying on its side unable to move, and then thrash its natural terror into exhausted submission. In short, the horse was forced to do what **we** wanted it to do by breaking its spirit. Then, after thousands of years of *this* practice, along came the "horse whisperer," Monte Roberts, who showed the world otherwise. By approaching a wild horse with good-will, trust, and the right kind of communication, exactly the same result could be achieved: a domesticated horse. But with two huge differences. First, neither he nor the horse experienced or expressed the least violence. And second, the horse took part in the process completely voluntarily, following its natural instinct to form a bond with a human being.

Thank goodness we are living in a time when old beliefs in aggression and force are finally being seen for what they are: links in a chain of human violence that is finally being broken.

This then, in brief, is the difference between exorcism and depossession. To be sure, this is a subject that merits a much longer treatment. My simple aim here has been to make a clear distinction between the two, so you will understand not just the humane effectiveness of depossession, but also how it is a far better expression of our newly emerging human and spiritual understanding.

Chapter VI

Aftermath and Integration

The Dawn of a New Era

Following depossession, a person may be like a nation that has lived under a long-standing dictator. When the dictator is finally toppled, there's an initial rush of new-felt freedom, but it can take time for people to fully feel it, and then learn to navigate the new freedoms that are available to them. In quite the same way, a person who is no longer experiencing the insidious influence of an intrusive spirit may gain a new freedom, yet experience a kind of inner void at the same time. This is quite understandable, since this influence, however negative it may have been, has been a psychological fixture, and one whose role in the person's life may not be clear-cut. In this chapter we will look at depossession as the dawn of a new era filled with fresh possibilities.

Near-term and Longer-term Benefits

In the last chapter, I shared some of the immediate effects of depossession. I'd now like discuss the kinds of things people feel in the weeks and months that follow. The most general near-term effect is that the person is more conscious of how their actions are affecting their lives. Destructive habits, and negative thoughts and feelings that they have indulged, dimly observed, or even observed without the capacity to resist, now stand out as arenas of choice and intention. These habits, of course, do not magically disappear with the absence of the invading spirit. However, with their reclaimed integrity, the person finally has a clear opportunity to exercise *their own will* in areas where it was continually challenged by - or even subordinate - to the will of the invasive spirit.

A good example of this is the young woman who was obsessed by the soldier who had died smoking a cigarette. Under his influence, she had "smoked like a chimney" in what felt to her like a nervous compulsion. She was now free of the soldier's influence, but the nicotine in her system, her motor habits, and her psychological dependence on smoking continued to exert a strong pressure upon her. Now, however, each time she reached for a cigarette, the 'battle between yes and no' was fought on an entirely different terrain. And without the unseen promptings of the young soldier, she was able to subdue this tormenting compulsion.

This same principle extends into the psychological and social realms. Take the example of an alcoholic whose drinking expressed the urge of an invasive spirit. Like the smoker reaching for her cigarettes, the drinker will also have to confront their habit of reaching for a bottle. And as they succeed in not drinking, they will do so at a price – namely the experience of the conflicting biochemical sensations that one feels when breaking an addiction. This struggle, of course, is not confined to whether or not they reach for the bottle. It also extends deep into their psychology, touching upon issues of responsibility and relationship, both of which are usually stressed by an addiction. Like any recovering alcoholic, they will need to find a new footing in their relationship to work, colleagues, friends, and family. What will be different, though, is that the root cause of their alcoholism has been removed, leaving only "peripheral issues," so to speak, to be confronted.

For others, the near-term benefits will involve no such complexity or struggle. A person who was subject to uncontrolled bouts of anger may find that this anger simply disappears. A person who was chronically anxious may feel that their anxiety has wonderfully abated. Physical complaints such as headaches, pressure in the chest, or poor digestion may likewise simply vanish. There can be other near-term benefits whose roots lie deep in the psyche and defy a linear explanation. In the healing of the human psyche, the release of one tension can trigger the release of other tensions or significant memories. There is a wonderful design to this healing capacity, which can take place in ways we cannot logically understand.

One client had come to me with multiple complaints. Though she had a close and problematic relationship to her mother, that was not one of them; she didn't even mention it. Two weeks after her depossession she had a dream, though as she put it, "it was more of a real experience than a dream." In this experience, "I found myself in the presence of my mother, but it was the presence of two psyches; we could not see each other physically. There was a chasm between us, though, and it was absolutely unbridgeable, whether by words, feelings, or thoughts – and certainly not by touch. The absoluteness of this chasm between us plunged me into unspeakable sorrow. I awoke from the dream feeling empty and bereft, a feeling that hung over me for much of the next day."

This client's dream, of course, could have been a metaphor for the severing of an unnatural psychic bond that she had with her mother. She felt at once that this experience was related to the depossession. And she was right, for I had seen that her energy field had been invaded while she was still in her mother's womb. Her entire life had been an uphill battle, as her vital energies were shared with an intrusive spirit. Fortunately, she trusted that from the barren ground of her emptiness, fresh green shoots of Life would grow forth. As indeed they did, as they do for so many of my clients. Again and again I am amazed at the resilience and healing capacity of the human soul, which, like a house plant that seems withered almost to death, can again grow into a green, healthy plant.

The longer-term benefits of depossession are difficult to trace with much sureness, since so many variables in a person's life are inextricably intertwined. When we address the spiritual cause of a physical affliction, for example, we may well produce a healing that cannot be understood in isolation. Take, for example, the physical state of a substance abuser. As a result of depossession, such a person may experience a distinct healing influence on their health, emotions, and relationships. If there has been organ degeneration, though, this may be irreversible, and subject to many other factors unrelated to the absence of the invasive spirit.

Looking Forward, Not Backward

Following depossession, it is important for the person to turn the page and begin a new chapter in their life. I stress this point because clients sometimes wish to interpret their possession, often unhelpfully.

How did I attract this? Who is to blame for this? What was this person like, who inhabited my body? What were the dynamics of our relationship? While I quite understand such natural concerns, I ask my clients to please drop whatever personal mythologies they might wish to create around their situation. I say this first of all, because they may well spin a story that is neither constructive nor true. And second, because they may reinforce some long-held belief about themselves that also serves no purpose. It is for this reason, too, that I usually don't tell the client all of the specific details that I have learned about the intrusive soul during my interaction with it.

Of course, depossession also heralds a new phase of healing for the client, a phase that may call for vigilance, purposeful action, and emotional care. And in this phase that follows, I stand beside my client, ready to assist them in any way possible, for as long as they find it helpful. Possession has affected my clients to different degrees. In one it was a nagging burden that they gamely struggled with, while living an outwardly normal life. In another, it was a powerful affliction that defaced the quality of their life. Thus, while the trajectories of different people's lives will differ following their depossession, what they have in common is a new possibility of spiritual growth.

Even without depossession, we know that growth involves the shedding of old patterns, the stretching of our self-concepts, and the integration of new or neglected inner resources. None of these things is either easy or automatic, and they all require a definite commitment on the part of the client. In every case, though, as the smoke clears from a life lived under the shadow of an uninvited guest, the sun can again shine in the client's life.

For this to happen, the client also needs to make a clean break from the "bad hand" they may think life has dealt them. Dwelling on one's "bad hand" is a good way to sabotage one's efforts to turn that into a "good hand." Even with the brilliant opportunity offered by the absence of the possessing spirit, the past can exert a considerable undertow that needs to be resisted, and eventually exhausted.

Hermann Hesse acutely observed that we tend to make philosophy out of our weaknesses. For this reason, I would counsel anyone who has undergone depossession to take stock of their catalogue of negative beliefs. It's hard, of course, to say which of these beliefs stem directly from possession, but no matter: this is a golden opportunity to make a great leap forward in **all** of one's psychology, not just the dark corner labeled "possession."

A second task is to integrate the new psychological and emotional material that emerges in the absence of the wandering soul's pernicious influence. Many people who have been depossessed have already experienced deep psychological changes in their lives. Following depossession, they may simply experience a welcome new phase of accelerated intensity. Others, who are less familiar with the terrain of inner upheaval and growth, will wish to avail themselves of new resources to help them through. Since people come to shamanic healing with different backgrounds and experience, they will reach out for help according to their inner needs and intuition.

Can a Person who has been Depossessed be Invaded Again?

The short answer is 'yes.' Unless a person resolves the power loss that made them vulnerable in the first place, it is entirely possible for them to become host to another wandering spirit. While depossession indeed offers a breakthrough opportunity, in real growth there are no "silver bullets." If the roots of one's power loss are not addressed, the opportunity afforded by depossession can dissipate. And if that happens, a person can once again become vulnerable to possession. This is why follow-up with shamanic healing is so important.

Follow-up with Shamanic Healing

Following depossession, one may certainly return to other healing resources one has cultivated, which have stood served one well in the past. This may range from religious practices and prayer, to yoga and meditation practices, to psychological awareness cultivated through the lens of various systems and perspectives. For many, growth takes a hybrid path in which one cobbles together healing work drawn from eclectic sources, listening always to one's inner voice.

It is important to remember that a person's possession would not have been possible if they had not experienced power loss. Even a successful depossession, then, still leaves a person with the same weakness they had prior to their possession. This is why soul retrieval and/or additional extraction typically need to accompany depossession, which is but one specialized aspect of shamanic healing. I also strongly suggest a number of shamanic treatments that are designed to address the specific needs of a person following depossession. These are practices for healing and growth that may be taught or guided by a shamanic practitioner, and are designed to bear fruit within the context of one's individual soul work. The aim of such shamanic practice is to make authentic contact with the roots of one's soul, and to align one's path with one's soul's purpose in coming to this life.

In this regard, the shaman has no status as a guru or religious figure, and is respected only for his or her knowledge, insight, and the favor they have found with the Compassionate Spirits. In this sense, a shamanic path is quite compatible with every other psychological or religious path, even as it has its own contributions that are unique. After I have performed depossession for a person who is unfamiliar with shamanism, I counsel that person to learn more about shamanic healing, and ultimately, to practice on their own. This follow-up can take several forms.

The foundation practice is the shamanic journey into non-ordinary reality, which can be done by almost anybody. While an experienced shaman takes very specific journeys in order to perform diagnoses, depossession, remove intrusions, and recover lost soul parts in soul retrieval, these all require specific training. That said, almost everyone has the capacity to journey in non-ordinary reality, where they can access useful and revelatory information, have uplifting and healing experiences, and establish a personal relationship with Power Animals and Spirit Guides. The benefits one can receive from this are endless. One can receive spiritual guidance, insights into challenges one faces in work, health, and relationships, personal healing, and new understandings about the natural world.

Thus, while the shaman may offer welcome relief in an acute situation, there is a wonderful world of self-development that one can explore for oneself. In this area too, Sandra Ingerman has written an excellent introductory book, entitled 'Shamanic Journeying.' It describes the many benefits one can receive from the practice of shamanic journeys, and is also a practical guide on how to do so. With the practice of journeying, one can develop one's own soul song and forge an authentic connection to Spirit, which can offer tremendous help in preserving and magnifying the gains one has made. To anyone interested in exploring Shamanism, I would recommend The Foundation for Shamanic Studies, and the courses of Sandra Ingerman. They both offer compelling and experiential workshops that one should consider attending. Since I am a co-founder of the Associazione Visione Sciamanica, with Rachele Giancaspro, I obviously endorse their workshops in Europe as well.

Shamanic Circles

Another way to support the healing process is to participate in a shamanic circle. A shamanic circle is a community of people who are pursuing shamanic studies and practices together, ideally under the leadership and guidance of an experienced shaman. By sharing with like-minded people, one can learn the varieties and possibilities of shamanic practices far more readily than one would on one's own. It can also be a wonderful source of inspiration, as one is exposed to influences and experiences that spring not from a verbal teaching or external form, but from the deep well-springs of spiritual experience, which is the birthright of every human being. As the leader of a shamanic circle, I have been gratified to see the members of my circle sink new roots into the depths of their being, and have also enjoyed the good-will and fellowship that goes with it. In all of this, there is also the great satisfaction of knowing that our heart-felt needs are in the hands of Spirit, working with and alongside us.

Every Cloud Does Have a Silver Lining

The healing of affliction has its truest significance in the larger movement of the soul, along vistas that are out of time. From this perspective, our phases of affliction and healing assume a very different meaning from those that are commonly assumed. To be sure, the sharing of depleted energies with an invasive spirit can compromise one's life, perhaps even greatly and painfully. This unfortunate event, though, may well determine the many arenas in which one's character and spiritual destiny are forged in this life. As Shakespeare wrote: "Sweet are the uses of adversity." Illness, addictions, or emotional challenges can all create a medium that compels a person to develop positive qualities, such as persistence, hope, faith, and a fruitful turning from the material world.

There is no form of struggle or suffering whose endurance and transformation cannot positively serve our growth. The psychologist Carl Jung describes this as *colpa felix*, which is Latin for a "fortunate fall:" an apparently negative event whose fruit is spiritually positive. While being "possessed" is definitely a difficult experience, I have seen that it serves many as the impetus to the development and acquisition of a strong spiritual rudder.

In the end, our life is what it is – be it healthy and successful, sickly and diminished, and everywhere in between. In whatever circumstance we find ourselves, we are here for a reason. It thus behooves each one of us to explore why we are here, and to remember who we truly are: spirits that have chosen to come into this physical state to experience joy, beauty, and all of the nurturing aspects of this stupendous creation, but also to experience tragedies, pain and the endless sadness inherent in the human condition. For it is the entire mix that enables us to grow, to understand, and to develop a caring compassion for for each member of the creation, and for the Earth that is our home.

Chapter VII

Shamanic Depossession -
A First-hand Account

This is an account of depossession that was written by a client of mine, who prefers to remain anonymous, and who graciously offered to share his experience in this book. I like it because it puts a human face on many of the themes I've presented in this book.

I Had a Real Problem

Though I had always scraped by, I clearly had a weak hold on life. In my teens I used drugs to excess. In my 20's I had an eating disorder, in my 30's I had chronic fatigue, and I had cancer in my 40's. In my 50's my health was okay, but I found myself regularly breaking down crying - here, there, and everywhere. I also had miserable nightmares – year after year. Something was wrong deep inside me.

Shamanism Wasn't for Me... or so I Thought

Getting desperate, I finally went to a psychic – for the first and only time in my life. She told me lots of things that were full of remarkable insight, and she put them in a big picture that was really inspiring. In the days that followed, though, the only thing she said that stuck with me was the term "soul retrieval." I couldn't even remember the context, though, and she didn't even say that this was a shamanic term. For two months I found myself chewing on these two words, till I finally found myself googling it. This, in turn, led to my search for a shaman. I wanted to find someone who could do this wonderful-sounding healing.

Until then, I had felt zero attraction to shamanism. The drums, rattles, and feathers all seemed just primitive. And my idea of spirituality did not include animal spirits and the like. All in all, I had a pretty dismissive attitude toward it. But feeling myself boxed in a corner, I was willing to try something different.

This newborn wish to find a shaman – which was strange even to myself – finally led me to call Peter.

A Promising First Contact

I don't like the telephone for personal things. I braced myself, though, and called Peter, and found myself pouring my heart out to him. To my great relief, he seemed to "hear" me exactly as I intended. Not only did he listen carefully, but he also said lots of things that really soothed my frayed nerves. Because I trusted Peter on the telephone, I was ready to trust shamanism.

I hadn't read much about shamanism, and Peter didn't have his web-site yet. I didn't know then, that flying blind, I had found someone with decades of experience who had trained with two leaders in the modern resurgence of shamanism, Michael Harner and Sandra Ingerman. I had met the real thing.

I Meet Peter

The trust I felt on the telephone only grew when I finally met Peter. He's a warm, earthy person who has a natural way about him that immediately put me at ease. Later, as we worked together, I found that while he gave me all the "sympathy" I needed, he was also very direct and workman-like. In short, he was professional, in the same way as, say, a doctor or therapist.

My Healing

Peter lived in a lovely home and his studio had windows that looked out on distant mountains. Along with a variety of Native American drums, rattles, and paintings, there were three highly detailed bronze statues. One was an eagle, one was a hawk, and the other an owl. This room was devoted to his practice, and as I had felt before with certain body-workers, the energy was heightened such that I knew I had entered a distinctly different environment.

We sat facing each other and pretty much picked up where our phone conversation had let off. I poured out more of my story, while he asked me questions. It felt really good to finally be giving full voice to my sufferings.

When I was finally talked out, Peter lit some wild sage in a large shell, encircled me in its smoke, and said several prayers and invocations for my healing. Not many people these days say prayers or invoke spiritual help out loud, and I was struck by the sincerity of how he did this. This was a man speaking from his heart who seemed confident he was being heard.

"I'd like to see you in four or five days," he said, when he was done. I was disappointed, for we hadn't performed my soul retrieval, whatever that might be. But I agreed at once to return, even though it meant four hours of driving and a lost day's pay.

Driving back four days later, I felt hugely conflicted. After days of anticipation, I was suddenly attacked by a host of negative thoughts.

"What are you doing?!" went my thoughts... "Who is this man? Do you have any idea what he could do to you? Turn back! Turn back!! Why are you putting yourself through this?! Go home. GO HOME NOW!"

I know the landscape of my mind pretty well, and the urgency of these thoughts was unusual and disturbing. I had to stop up my ears, grip the steering wheel, keep my foot on the accelerator, and plow onwards – all the time feeling really stressed by this.

I made it. But sitting opposite Peter again, my emotions were barely in check. We talked some more about my sufferings... however... on the phone and in our first session he had given me free rein, but this time **he** held the reins. He asked me very specific questions about how I was suffering, and how I felt about it. And he parsed my answers very carefully; he didn't just "listen." Each time I described my situation with negativity or with judgment, he coaxed me into rephrasing it in a more positive way. We ended up recasting my life-story in a way that was less personal and less negative. I also felt that he was not talking to **me** as he had the first time. It felt as if we were enacting a script that had some kind of aim I wasn't privy to.

At one point I began to feel as if the room no longer had a ceiling, that the room opened out into endless space. I also saw that while Peter was engaging me, he was also engaged elsewhere, a perception I have had before with people entering deeper inner spaces.

Things then happened very fast, in a sequence I can't entirely remember. I recall that my emotional state was becoming unbearable. I remember Peter guiding me down onto a mat on the floor, to perform a healing, during which an emotional catharsis then took me over completely – and I mean **completely**. Hot, desperate tears welled up from deep inside me, wave after wave, each more intense than the last.

When this eruption of emotion seemed to have finally run its course, it was followed by neither calmness nor relief. For no sooner had this one strong emotion passed than another very different one took its place.

Angry declarations now issued forth from my depths, as I pounded the floor with my fists.

"I've never lived!" I declared, over and over and over again. "I've never lived!!" I said, with a strange force and certainty. Indeed, I had never said anything in my life with such definiteness, which seemed to come from my very bones.

After what seemed as long while, the storm subsided. I opened my eyes. The sculptures of the eagle and owl loomed above me. Peter was sitting in his chair looking down on me.

It was then that he told me... in our conversation about this experience, he revealed that my body had been inhabited by an entity who had been feeding upon my energies for my entire lifetime. He had persuaded the entity to move on. It was gone now. I was free of it. This took place when I had felt the space opening out, and the entity had spoken with Peter using my own voice. It turned out that Peter had also, in his original journey on my behalf, received an indication from Spirit that he should perform a soul retrieval. It was this that had taken place on the mat, and this that had filled me with such powerful energy and feeling.

So - not only had I received the soul retrieval I had come for, but I'd been depossessed, as well!

🦅

Next Steps

Did I see my life-long companion, the entity? No, I didn't. After all, that's why we have shamans! Had I ever sensed this "companion?" No, but while I did not suspect a spiritual invasion of this sort, I intuitively knew that some sort of distinct force was actively sapping my energy. And considering my experience leading up to the session and during the session, not to mention the really deep healing that followed in its wake, it is easy for me accept that this had been the case.

I was full of questions. Who had been feeding off my energy all these years? Was it a man or woman? What was he or she like? I was eager for details that would explain many of the unhappy sides of my life. Here, though, my sympathetic shaman drew the line. "Move forward," he said. "Forget about it. It's gone now. Just go have a great life."

I then had a series of follow-up sessions with Peter, in which he taught me how to journey. Both in Peter's presence, and also on my own, at home, I then had a number of healing experiences that were every bit as strong and magical as that first experience. Among them, I experienced the reality of Power Animals, which was something I'd never even thought of before, as well as the truly dramatic healing power of Spirit. Ever since this period of intense healing, my life has become a small miracle, as the life force that had been shut down all my life is now coming through to me. I am experiencing it in my bones, my spine, and in my energetic sense of myself.

In indigenous cultures, the shaman often acts as a kind of psychologist and minister. In the three years since I first met him, I have often been grateful for the insight that Peter has shared with me. I have had desperate moments when his reassuring presence on the telephone was a godsend, and I've never felt the least waning in his commitment to me. Our relationship has been deeply human, right from the start.

Three years ago, I could not have written these words.

I would also have been doubtful if I had read them.

Thank God we can go beyond our own limitations and find the Good that we want and deserve.

Resources for Further Study

Here is a list of some of my favorite books on both shamanism and ideas related to the shamanic world-view. There are countless books I would like to list, but let's call this a good starting point.

Books are a wonderful way of communicating, but I would like to remind my reader that true Shamanic revelation comes from direct contact with our own compassionate Helping Spirits and our ever-present Allies. In short, books are the jumping-off point for first-hand experience, which is available to everyone.

Essential Sacred Writings from Around the World
by Mircea Eliade, Harper San Francisco
This is a compilation of sacred texts assembled by the famed pioneer in introducing shamanic traditions worldwide to modern men and women.

The Way of the Shaman
by Michael Harner, Harper San Francisco
This modern classic, written by the founder of the Foundation for Shamanic Studies, combines the rigor of a researcher with first-hand experience of living shamanic traditions in explaining the essential core of shamanic practice.

Cave and Cosmos – Shamanic Encounters with Another Reality
by Michael Harner, North Atlantic Books, Berkeley, California

Drawing from a lifetime of personal shamanic experiences and more than 2,500 reports of Westerner's experiences during shamanic ascension, Harner highlights the striking similarities among their discoveries, which indicate that the heavens and spirits they've encountered do indeed exist. He also provides instructions on his innovative core-shamanism techniques, so that readers, too, can ascend to heavenly realms, seek spirit teachers, and return later, at will, for additional healing and advice.

The Encyclopedia of Shamanism
Vols. 1 & 2, by Christina Pratt, The Rosen Publishing Group - New York
As an encyclopedia, these books are of course fairly dry, but they're filled with good information on a wide range of subjects. Best of all, there's lots of cross-referencing in bold-face, which makes it easy and profitable to jump around from topic to topic.

Soul Retrieval
by Sandra Ingerman, Harper San Francisco
A wonderful introduction to the theory and practice of soul retrieval, filled with personal accounts, and written with a warm heart.

Shamanic Journeying
by Sandra Ingerman, Sounds True
Another wonderful introduction, this time to the practice of journeying, the basic shamanic practice that opens the door to non-ordinary reality.

Medicine for the Earth
by Sandra Ingerman, Three Rivers Press
Better known for her shamanic teaching, Sandra Ingerman here combines her deep understanding of ecology with shamanic practices, to help us see how spirituality can be brought to bear practically upon the natural world.

Weather Shamanism
by Nan Moss with David Corbin, Inner Traditions/Bear & Co.
In today's world of computerized weather forecasters, this is an

eye-opening look at the variety of weather beings, angels, spirits and helpers who are a real, but invisible part of the weather we experience daily.

Soul Rescuers
by Terry and Natalia O'Sullivan, Thorsons
An in-depth look at many of the issues addressed in this book, such as the afterlife, reincarnation, and shamanic realities in different cultural traditions.

The Spirit Book
by Alan Kardec, Brotherhood of Life, Inc.
Kardec was a French scientist of the 19th century who systemized what is known as Spiritism. A mature consideration of such important topics as the immortality of the soul, the nature of spirits and their relationship to the living, moral law, and much more.

The Dreamer's Book of the Dead
by Robert Moss
A book that takes us beyond our ordinary consensus view of reality by exploring how the dead communicate to us through dreams. Based on massive research that takes us into the deeper currents of pre-Christian spirituality.

The I Ching
Princeton University Press
This classic of ancient China represents a system of divination that inspired not just the philosophy and cosmology of China, but millions of people world-wide, with its wisdom of "a world of changes."

Dreamways of the Iroqouis
by Rober Moss, Destiny Books
A startling and original view of the role of dreams among the Iroquois, based upon the author's first-hand revelations. Best of all, he shares how this knowledge can serve us today, just as it has served Native Americans since time immemorial.

Lakota Belief and Ritual
Edited by Raymond J. DeMallie and Elane A. Jahner, University of Nebraska Press
Narratives of Lakota holy men are presented verbatim in translation, without analysis. We thus receive a direct "feel" for Lakota spirituality that is quite different from the commentaries of even the best-intentioned outsiders.

Shaman Healer Sage
Harmony Books - Alberto Villoldo
A wonderful introduction to shamanism, due to its depth of understanding, and ability to explain seemingly mystical and magical practices in a way that is understandable to those versed in many other forms of spirituality.

The Four Agreements
by Don Miguel Ruiz, Amber-Allen Publishing Inc.
This skinny little book by a modern Toltec shaman became an international best-seller, for it speaks simply and from the heart about a wise and moral approach to life.

Destiny of Souls
by Michael Newton, Llewellyn Publications
A psychotherapist takes a detailed look at the life of the soul in its many phases: before, during, and after this present lifetime, and its relationship to the larger spirit world.

The Seat of the Soul
by Gary Zukav, Fireside
An exploration of many aspects of how we can move from the confines of our five senses to having the experience of being a multi-sensory spirit in a body.

The Farther Reaches of Human Nature
by A.H. Maslow, An Esalen Book
An honest, probing consideration of what it means to be human, and what it means to move beyond the psychological limitations we have accepted as simply "the way life is."

The Land Of Remorse
by Ernesto De Martino, Free Association Book
Written by a pioneer of ethnopsychiatry, this is a study of tarantism, a specialized form of possession known in Southern Italy. I like the way this book determines the shamanic reality of a practice that might easily be dismissed as irrational superstition.

Fools Crow - Wisdom and Power
by Thomas E. Mails, Council Oak Books - San Francisco
The words and wisdom of a remarkable Sioux holy man, who died in 1989 at the age of 99. A classic of Native American spirituality that speaks straight to the heart.

Black Elk Speaks
by John G. Neihardt, University of Nebraska Press
A sympathetic portrait of the great Lakota holy man, whose patient wisdom and compassion come through with great strength.

The Power of Myth
by Joseph Campbell, Broadway Books
A highly accessible introduction to Campbell's lifelong exploration of how myths have served mankind, and can serve each of us in our individual journeys.

Historical Atlas of World Mythology
Volumes 1 & 2, by Joseph Campbell
As the title implies, a compendium of information about mythology, and a fine resource for anyone engaged in shamanic practice or dream work.

The Unquiet Dead – A Psychologist Treats Spirit Possession
by Dr. Edith Fiore
A great book about her own experience as a psychologist and past life therapist who discovers and treats spirit attachment.

The Origin of Satan
by Elaine Pagels

Written by the popular and critically acclaimed author of The Gnostic Gospels, this is a dramatic interpretation of the role of Satan in the Christian tradition. With deep academic knowledge infused into great story-telling, she explores Christianity's shadow side, in which the gospel of love gives way to irrational hatred that continues to haunt both Christians and non-Christians alike.

Suggested Web-sites

www.shamanswisdom.org
This is the web-site for my personal practice as a shamanic practitioner.

www.visionesciamanica.it
(in Italian) – The web-site for shamanic studies conducted by myself and my Italian colleagues.

www.shamanism.org
The web-site of the Foundation for Shamanic Studies, where I received my training.

www.sandraingerman.com
The web-site for Sandra Ingerman, an authentic shaman and colleague whose books are recommended above.

www.betsybergstrom.com
The web-site for Betsy Bergstrom, the shaman whose quotation in Chapter 1 gives fine insight into the "partnership" between the host and their invisible phantom influence.

www.traditioninaction.org
The web-site where one can find the liturgy used in the rites of exorcism of the Catholic Church.

Printed in Great Britain
by Amazon

26056532R00066